Best wishes to
Fred Crane

Don Ried



# *Jazz Memories*

# Biography

Dan Bied was born Nov. 21, 1925. He is a graduate of Burlington Junior College, in Iowa, and attended a two-week seminar at Columbia University's School of Journalism.

He was news director at KBUR in 1956 and was a reporter, photographer and deputy editor at The Burlington Hawk Eye from 1957 through 1967. In recent years he was editor of the house organ at the Iowa Army Ammunition Plant and has written columns for The Des Moines Register, The Des Moines County News and The Shopper's Spree. His articles on jazz have appeared in The Mississippi Rag and the St. Louis Jazz Club's newsletter.

Bied is a member of the International Association of Jazz Record Collectors (IAJRC) and the 106th Infantry Division Association. He and his wife, the former Millie Stodgell, enjoy travel, the St. Louis Cardinals and, of course, jazz.

His previous books include: "Burlington Once Upon a Time," "Encore," "Trio," "Backstage Burlington," "Hell On Earth," "History of West Burlington," "My Kind of Town" and "Memories."

# *Jazz Memories*



Dan Bied

Craftsman Press, Inc.
Burlington, Iowa
1994

# Credits

Cover photo: Paul Gonsalves takes a solo on "Praise God and Dance" during Duke Ellington's sacred music concert at Burlington, Ia., on Feb. 25, 1971.

Front cover photo and shot of Duke Ellington with Cootie Williams were taken by Mike Hatt. Photos of Benny Goodman with Peggy Lee and BG playing a trumpet are from Arsene Studios. Photo of the author with Goodman was taken by Popsie Randolph. Photos of Wardell Gray at the Armar Ballroom and Harry James at the Burlington Auditorium were by Dawson Brown. Photo of Hillard Brown with Art Hodes was by The Burlington Hawk Eye. Photo of Earl Hines was provided by Stanley Dance. Photo of Louis Armstrong with Leonard Brooks was by Rich Van Cleef. Back cover photo was by Bob Wilson. All other photos were taken by the author.

---

"Jazz Memories" is dedicated to Bette Scott, who launched her younger brother's love affair with jazz when she told him about Bix.

Special thanks are extended to Stanley Dance, for his encouragement and advice, and to all the jazz musicians, from Armstrong to Zentner, who inspired the text.

# Contents

# Preface

"Jazz Memories" relates my experiences as a devoted fan since 1942. The concept of this book only dates back 12 years, however. It was in 1982 that I ran across "The Otis Ferguson Reader" in a Chicago store. The collection of Ferguson's writings, mostly about jazz, impressed me as being the type of thing I eventually wanted to write, using my observations in place of his and adding my own photos.

Ferguson, as many jazz followers know, became something of a cult figure when his pithy essays about the swing era, with emphasis on Benny Goodman's band and the lingering genius of Bix Beiderbecke, created a stir in The New Republic. He was still writing whatever crossed his mind until, as a merchant seaman, he was killed in a World War II explosion off Italy.

What I wrote was based, to large extent, on such memorabilia as newspaper clippings, magazine articles, concert programs and my own notes from the past half-century. It took some editing and the addition of ingredients from the top of my head to stir it all into a book.

I opted to do "Jazz Memories" as a series of self-contained articles rather than a chronology, a diary account or a continuing story. Care was taken to avoid distraction from other themes. There are no sub-plots about social issues, etc. Just jazz, as I remember it from the past 52 years.

The book's timing was triggered, in part, by "The Duke Ellington Reader," edited by Mark Tucker and published in 1993 by the Oxford University Press.

The impressive Ellington book includes an article written by the Duke for Down Beat in 1939 in which he noted: "A musician seldom makes a good critic, since he naturally has his own ideas of how music should be played. Accordingly, the musician should accept the fact that a critic is not necessarily required to play an instrument in order to properly fulfill the job of critic. In fact, the critic is more likely to deliver impartially if he is not musically talented."

I am not a musician. My only instruments are the typewriter and the camera. I am a reporter, more than a critic, and certainly a serious fan of jazz with roots in the swing era. I do, of course, have some likes, some dislikes and some opinions I'm not too bashful to express.

To elaborate: it does not bother me that jazz ranks behind country and rock music in mass popularity across the United States. But it is unfortunate, I think, that jazz enjoys more status as an art form in Europe, and perhaps in the Far East, than in the US. When played at its best, jazz is as worthwhile as the best in classical music. So it should be as revered in America, where it was born, as it is in Amsterdam or Tokyo. "Jazz Memories," which reflects some toil and financial risk, is my small contribution to the cause.

This book is a departure from my eight earlier soft-backs which dealt with "the good old days" in Burlington, Ia., where I was born. My early musical inspirations included jazz by Fats Waller, Erskine Hawkins, Count Basie and others heard over the radio in my dad's drug store. The station I usually listened to, WCAZ, played more jazz than country music even though it was broadcasting from the small town of Carthage, Ill., in the cornbelt.

Some of my writing output, linked to an era when I graduated from my hometown's soda fountains to its taverns and lounges, first got into print during my 11 years as a reporter and occasional editor with The Burlington Hawk Eye. While my sidekicks longed for fire trucks to chase I yearned for a one-nighter around Southeast Iowa by such royalty as the Duke, the Count or Earl Hines.

Memories of two appearances by Hines are, in fact, among those prompting me to do this book. I wrote about the time the band came to Burlington in 1942 for a dance and also the legendary pianist's three-week gig at a local night club three decades later.

My sister suggested that I could have titled the book "Jazz Odyssey." It does, after all, include reports on jazz since the early forties in my travels to London, Paris, New York, Chicago, Boston, St. Louis, Iowa City, Sarasota, Newport Beach - etc. There is also an item dealing with a jazz cruise in the Caribbean, one of five "floating festivals" my wife and I enjoyed in the eighties.

The book's recollections include the Sunday afternoon at Sweet Basil when Doc Cheatham was joined by Wynton Marsalis and Harry Edison in a spirited jam session, seeing the Ellington band at the Panther Room in 1942 and my "audience" with the King of Swing on July 2, 1948.

Some of the text recalls my friendships with such jazz notables as Art Hodes and Al Hall. I included excerpts from interviews and performance reviews involving Basie, Goodman, Ellington, Stan Kenton, Woody Herman and other jazz "names." There are, to round things out, reports about such hallowed jazz venues as the Metropole, Pizza Express, Ronnie Scott's and Eddie Condon's.

The result is a "labor of love" kind of book that reflects jazz I've heard during six decades. I will be satisfied, to risk another cliche, if it is considered "an artistic success."

# *Big Bands*
# *&*
# *Jazz Legends*

# On the Road

Any jazz fan old enough to remember the swing era, from the not-so-roaring thirties until after World War II, has some favorite memories.

It was nothing, it seemed, to drive 100 or more miles to see Goodman, Kenton, Ellington, Basie or the Dorseys perform "in the flesh."

Some guys brought their own bottles to get high while others felt intoxicated enough when they heard, and actually saw, Ben Webster blow his torrid solo on "Cottontail" as only he could do it. Or Ziggy Elman tooting through the roof on "And the Angels Sing." Those hep to the jive were usually up front leaning over the footlights.

I was too young, just 16 the day Pearl Harbor was bombed, to get in on all of it.

An older pal entered his final days still remembering the thrill of Tommy Dorsey's Clambake Seven with Johnny Mince on clarinet, surging tenorman Bud Freeman and, best of all to him, the jazzy vocalisms of Edythe Wright. "I still remember TD," he'd say, "from 1937 . . ."

Another gent told me several times about the afternoon in 1938 when Bob Crosby, driving a Cadillac roadster, gave him a lift from Iowa City to Burlington. He was in the rumbleseat behind the head Bob Cat and his one-of-a-kind pianist, Bob Zurke. Even without any music it was a memorable event, one my friend still talks about whenever there's mention of jazz.

Once, in 1929, there was a dance at a Burlington ballroom with Fletcher Henderson's band. Jimmy Harrison may have been there, I guess, along with Kaiser Marshall and even Coleman Hawkins, "the Bean." But I slept through it, at age four, above my dad's store.

Henderson returned twice, though, during World War II. I'll never forget, in particular, seeing the band on May 13, 1943. An ammunition plant near Burlington had added to our awareness of global events. The band didn't have any well-known players but it was doing just great until the power went off.

The auditorium, with hundreds of people in it, went pitch black. There was a long delay. The moment the outage was fixed Fletcher's male vocalist, a booming baritone, went to the microphone and sang "When the Lights Go On Again All Over the World." Hardly a time for dry eyes.

Sonny Dunham, a virtuoso known for his brilliant trumpet solo on "Memories of You," brought an impressive band to town the same year. After hitting some awesome high notes on his silver horn he picked up a trombone, an instrument few if any nearby jazz buffs knew he played. He proceeded to do a stratospheric sliphorn solo on "You're Blase," alternating with his trumpet. It left some front-row mouths ajar.

Alvino Rey was in Burlington with a solid outfit and, of course, his zinging guitar. The band was sailing along on a brassy jump tune when, suddenly, everything stopped. Rey hit a single, jarring note on his amplified box that sent a shiver up my back. Up or down, I remember it "like yesterday."

Shep Fields checked in with a "Rippling Rhythm" orchestra that included a rhythm section, seven or eight saxophonists, including the versatile Romeo Penque, but no brass. Even without trumpets the music was still very good.

In the winter of 1942 a not-yet-chubby kid from Chicago named Mel Torme sang and cut up at the Burlington Auditorium. He was with a band led by Chico Marx, who clowned around at "the 88."

**Memorial Auditorium**

BURLINGTON, IOWA.

**THURSDAY, MAY 13th**

| DANCE TICKETS To Colored People ONLY | BALCONY SEATS |
|---|---|
| Advance .......$1.25, Inc. Tax | Open to The General Public. |
| At Door .......$1.40, Inc. Tax | 65c, Including Tax. |

Tickets on Sale at Sutter's Drug Store, Witte's Drug Store, Dehner's Cigar Store, Byrnsie's Cigar Store, Denniston Insurance Agency, Dixie Tavern and Bergman's Drug Store in Ft. Madison, Ia.

Mail orders to H. E. Cooper, Memorial Auditorium, Burlington, Ia., will receive prompt attention. Enclose self-addressed envelope and remittance.

Chico had a very able swing band with George Wettling on drums and Phil Napoleon, who was 41 at the time, taking the hot solos on trumpet. Marx was replaced by a more sedate pianoman when the band played dance tunes or swing. Torme was around 17 at the time. He looked even younger but performed with all the gleeful ease of a budding Bing Crosby.

Boomie Richman, a tenorman who played furiously enough to pick up where Freeman left off, made up with gusto what he might have lacked in finesse. His long, heated solos with TD were almost as remarkable to watch as they were to hear. I can remember his fingers going like pistons as his cheeks puffed up and turned red. I wondered if he might explode.

This was around 1947. That year, in Atlantic City, it was my pleasure to see two bands the same night on the famous Steel Pier. They were led by Randy Brooks, who had been a top-notch first trumpeter with Les Brown and Claude Thornhill, and the legendary Jean Goldkette.

Brooks' popularity had soared with a major hit, "Harlem Nocturne," in the mid-forties. His book also included an array of jump tunes played in deft, swinging fashion. Goldkette, who was 48 at the time, had become famous in the twenties with a big orchestra that featured Bix Beiderbecke, Joe Venuti, clarinetist Danny Polo and the Dorsey brothers at one time or another. His band at Atlantic City wasn't in that realm but it provided first-class dance music. I was surprised to see Goldkette directing a band, figuring he was either retired or dead.

The crowd that night, during a July heat wave, was immense. The floor was just off the boardwalk with its salt water taffy shops, hucksters selling souvenirs and enough people to populate Bangladesh. The Steel Pier was a sprawling complex with theaters, carnival rides, restaurants, bars and hundreds of good-looking women. My pal and I "had a ball."

Back in Burlington, Tommy Dorsey showed up that fall with Elman and Charlie Shavers in his trumpet section plus a young, impressive clarinetist named Buddy DeFranco. It was that night, I think, when a couple of drunks got into a fight in the men's room and TD, who was just passing by, yanked them apart. He could have ignored the brawl, but Tommy wasn't the type to duck a good scrap.

Stan Kenton, an opposite type, was helping a teen-ager straighten his tie in a Quad Cities restroom one night as I entered to join the urinal line.

Another time, in the late forties, the Kenton band ended a one-nighter at the Ottumwa Armory with an impromptu salvo of Dixieland. I don't recall what caused it, probably just someone's request or dare. But the most progressive band in the land played twenties-style jazz for, as far as I know, the first and last time via such modernists as Buddy Childers, Kai Winding, Bob Cooper and Shelly Manne. I'll swear on a stack of Down Beats that it really happened!

Also in Ottumwa, the first of Woody Herman's numerous herds arrived one night about two hours late. Red Norvo didn't get his apparatus on stage until after 11 p.m. He looked beat, as though he could have dozed off at the vibes. They went through the motions, more or less, but still played fine jazz.

In Cedar Rapids, the Harry James band was greeted by a gent with a movie camera equipped with a huge spotlight who spent much of the evening prowling around the stand. He was within a few feet of the befuddled Music Makers when, finally, altoman Willie Smith figured out how to cope. He picked out one of his charts, pointed to the title and waved the sheet around for the benefit of the band: "I'm Beginning To See the Light."

This was all great fun. But my most precious big band memory goes back to around 1948 when Cootie Williams and his crew played a one-nighter at Quincy, Ill. I was in junior college at the time and took a friend, who cared little about jazz, along for the ride. If nothing else, I figured, he could be my "designated driver" on the way home.

The venue was a big, dilapidated pavilion that looked like something we might have seen in a movie with Jimmy Cagney and Joan Blondell. The place was already buzzing when Dick and I arrived, an hour or so ahead of Cootie and his band.

The dance began late, but no one got too antsy. There was plenty to drink and, as someone probably said: "The night is young!"

Finally, things got rolling around 10 o'clock. The band opened its fire with an uptempo "Stompin' at the Savoy." Not too fast, just right.

They played chorus after chorus, then played more. They wailed, with the soloists parading to the microphone one after another. Honking saxes, roaring brass. They played "Savoy" for 30 or more minutes, then followed up with something louder. "Gatortail," I think.

People kept coming, shoving their way in wherever they could. By 11, it was so crowded a guy could have passed out and not hit the floor.

Some places still had "color line" policies in the late forties. I mentioned to my friend that we were the only whites in the building, except for two cops. No one cared. Certainly not us. Integration had arrived, at least in the realm of jazz.

We stayed past midnight. It was a 90-mile drive home and we both had classes the next day, if that mattered. The drive, over a serpentine road much narrower than today's Hwy. 96, wasn't much of a worry at age 22.

The jazz that night still comes to mind now and then. I can hear it, almost. I can "see" one of the trumpeters blowing from the stand, then walking to a table on the dance floor, with the band still playing, for a highball. He was wearing a dark blue suit, with broad lapels, a white shirt and a tiger-stripe tie.

Cootie Williams wasn't a demanding boss, at least not that night a few years after WW-2. Maybe he was a poor businessman. His band didn't make it too long, falling victim to "the times."

But it could wail.

# Earl Hines

I was nearly breathless waiting for the curtain to go up in the Burlington Auditorium on May 29, 1942.

It was a Friday night, if that's important, and Earl Hines was in town with his 17-piece band.

After being smitten by *le jazz hot* the previous winter, it was my first opportunity to see and hear a famous orchestra in action. Certainly, Hines had one of the best.

"Fatha Hines," someone yelled from behind the curtain as it started to go up. "Fatha Hines!" The brass shouted, the saxes blew, the bass viol boomed and the cymbals crashed. Hines, a handsome gent who was just Jack Benny's age at the time, cut loose with a flurry of notes at the grand piano.

Everything was grand that night. It was a festive occasion with some of the "hepcats" traveling 100 or more miles to see the Hines band.

I remember a group of black teen-agers, in particular. They were dressed up in bright sport jackets and several of them wore big, floppy caps. They were from the Quad Cities and vied for sartorial honors with a white guy from Burlington attired in a cream-colored zoot suit. With reet pleats, of course.

The event was advertised as a dance for "colored people only," in keeping with local custom. Tickets were $1 in advance and $1.40 at the door, including tax. Balcony seats, available to whites, were 65 cents. (The building was erected as a WPA project in 1938, to seat more than 2,000 people, and the wood-block floor "exploded" now and then in hot weather. Air conditioning was installed in 1962, fixing that problem. The building suffered extensive damage during the 1993 flood but is still considered by many to be "the crown jewel" among municipal assets).

Billy Eckstine, at age 29, was the star among the sidemen as he played in the trumpet section and sang a dozen or more times during the night. Along with his boss, he was good looking enough to be a movie star.

Eckstine's voice was deep, polished and downright wonderful. He was as talented as any of the big band male singers, including Sinatra and Dick Haymes. It was a treat to be there as he performed some of the numbers he had done on Bluebird records. "The Jitney Man," "Somehow," "Stormy Monday Blues" and "Skylark."

There was a vocal group, probably Madeline Greene and the Three Varieties, backing Eckstine on "I Got It Bad" and some other tunes. (I should remember it if Sarah Vaughan was with Hines that night).

Charles ("Truck") Parham, who returned to Burlington in 1965 for a gig with Art Hodes, was the bass player, as I recall it. Franz Jackson, a Chicagoland jazz great over the years, told me a few years ago that he was in the sax section when Hines toured in the spring of 1942. (I might also remember Charlie Parker if he had been with the band that night).

It was a very able band, though not staffed with "name" performers in the tradition of Ellington, Basie or Cab Calloway. Hines provided much of the spark himself, doing Mel Powell's tribute to him, "The Earl." The band played "The Father Jumps" and "Second Balcony Jump." I was in the second balcony that night, but only jumped with joy.

Hines was no stranger to jazz fans in Burlington, but was playing in our town for the first time. He had performed at the Grand Terrace on South Park Avenue in Chicago during the thirties. Some people I knew had seen "Fatha" at the Grand Terrace. His broadcasts over WMAQ and WENR were heard in Burlington, some 220 miles away, as well as more distant points.

I remember hearing Hines do his boogie woogie version of "St. Louis Blues" over the radio. "Don't quit now, dad.

Play 'til 1951!" There were two nightly broadcasts over WMAQ to the East and, an hour later, over WENR to the West. Hines scaled down to a combo after the war, as the big bands were curtailed by a combination of high costs and the upsurge in musical drivel.

He was inactive part of the time but recorded the acclaimed Little Theater concert in 1964 and, as early as 1971, began to etch a superb collection of Ellington tunes.

The boxed set of LPs was released by Book of the Month Records shortly before Hines died, in 1983.

Late in 1972, Hines had brought a combo to Burlington to play for three weeks at a new night club, called Pzazz!, that had been built by John Winegard, a jazz fan who became a very successful producer of TV antennas. I was a frequent customer at the Pzazz! complex as John's bandstand hosted nightly shows in the Las Vegas vein and, on occasion, jazz combos and big bands. The appearance by Hines was a distinguished achievement and the combo drew appreciative crowds.

I wasn't writing for publication at that time and, with his permission, am enhancing my "Jazz Memories" with the following report Lloyd Maffitt wrote for The Hawk Eye on Dec. 5, 1972:

"A living legend of the jazz keyboard who has a background in classical music opened an extended gig at Burlington's Pzazz! last night. Fatha Hines' quintet has Marva Josie out front as vocalist, also classically trained, and Jimmy Lewis on cello, an unusual instrument in jazz. Tiny Grimes plays guitar and Ray Mosca dominates the drums.

"Pittsburger Hines (christened Earl Kenneth) studied in local schools and switched to jazz because 'in those days there were no opportunities for Negroes in classical music.' His mastery of the piano is so total that he can make even that most simple minded of tunes, 'Tea for Two,' sound like a sonata.

"Hines will be 67 on Dec. 28, but he looks 20 years younger, a fact he attributes to drinking prune juice regularly, bowling and working out thrice weekly at the YMCA.

"Hines, who describes himself as 'a down-to-earth fellow who loves people,' played with Louis Armstrong in the twenties, with the Hot Five, and later with his own big bands.

"He devotes 2½ months each year to cultural tours abroad for the US State Department and has been cited and applauded on every continent and behind the Iron Curtain. He was voted into the Down Beat Hall of Fame in 1965.

"When he concludes his Burlington engagement, Hines will take a three-week vacation. 'We'll have a family reunion; I have two daughters, Janear - my wife's name is Janie and we took the first three letters of her name and the first three of mine to make it - and Tosca, who's majoring in dance and drama at UCLA. Our home is at Oakland.'

"Hines recalled an occasion when 'The college kids at Vail, Colo., came to see me in New York. I was playing at a new spot called the Half Note and they begged me to play a concert in Vail, and I said I would.'

"The pianist said he has no favorites in the size of ensemble or numbers. 'Whatever I'm doing at the moment I like best,' he stated. He sees little future for big bands, however, because of the great cost.

"In his youth, Hines revealed, he was an amateur boxer who used to work out, strictly for fun, with Joe Louis. He expressed amused contempt for the many untalented people who temporarily catch the public's fancy in these days of instant celebrity.

"'When Duke Ellington and I were young,' he said, 'you were screened through the clubs and small theaters. You had to prove yourself before you got a chance at the big time. Now some guy can beat on a dishpan and they'll cut a record of it. But these people are forgotten in a year or two. They're too gimmicky, and gimmicks are no good in the long run. The public catches onto the fact that these people are using gimmicks to try to cover up the fact that they're phonies.'"

Highlights of Hines' opening night program included "Slaughter On Tenth Avenue," done as a piano-drum duet between himself and Mosca; "Just Friends," a Hines-Mosca-Lewis number; and Miss Josie's openers, "S'Wonderful," by Gershwin, and "You'd Be So Easy To Love."

I attended several performances by the combo, of course, and was pleased by every note. Hines asked for the audience to be quiet once, during a weekend show when the Tiger Pit was filled. Everyone cooperated and we all enjoyed the hour-long set.

NOTE: The last time I saw Hines was at the Ritz-Carlton in Chicago, during 1975. His combo featured the talented saxman, Eric Schneider, and drummer Eddie Graham. Hines, puffing on a big stogie, was outstanding at the keyboard as he played some of the tunes that established him as the greatest of all jazz pianists.

Hines was accused of abandoning jazz for a "vaudeville" approach in his later years. But I am convinced that jazz is entertainment, played at times for people who are not devout students of the art form. Ellington and Armstrong were also entertainers, as was Fats Waller. Hines did nothing in bad taste. It was my assumption that his "commercial" leanings helped keep his music alive.

# Duke Ellington

During an interview with Duke Ellington in 1964 it seemed appropriate, as his sidemen were drifting back to the bandstand, to toss him a bouquet.

"That's a wonderful orchestra you have," I remarked just before a roll from Sam Woodyard's drum signaled the end of the band's "coffee break."

"Thank you," the Duke responded. "I wish I could afford it."

Keeping his band intact was an ongoing challenge for Ellington as salaries escalated and his travel costs kept going up. He spent much of his time on the road doing one-nighters, often in small towns.

His first visit to Burlington had been on May 25, 1940, in the era of $1 dance tickets and records that sold for less than 50 cents. Members of his band that Saturday night included, I believe, such greats as Ben Webster, Johnny Hodges, Barney Bigard, Harry Carney, Rex Stewart and Sonny Greer. I was only 14 at the time and too interested in cowboy movies and model planes to notice jazz.

It was different in August, 1942, when my dad took me to Chicago to see the Cubs, his favorite team. I was a full-fledged jazz nut by then and, though he leaned toward Al Jolson and light waltzes, he took me to the Panther Room in the Hotel Sherman to see the Ellington show.

The Panther Room was an exciting place, located on the lower level of the hotel in what was called the College Inn. It was the first night club I had seen, other than in the movies. I remember a long bar at the left as we entered the complex, with a decor that included a lot of bamboo and other light-colored woods. The main room was dark, except for the spotlights. There was a small floor in front of the stand, which was across from the bar. It was used for floor shows and, I believe, for dancing.

The waiters, mostly black men, wore turbans and impressed me with their deft footwork as they delivered "flaming sword" entrees and other orders in the crowded room. "The Flaming Sword," which was recorded in Chicago in 1940, happened to be one of my first Ellington discs.

Chauncey Haughton had succeeded Bigard as the band's clarinet soloist. He did not fill Barney's shoes, perhaps. But I enjoyed him that night because he played more like a swing era jazzman, while Bigard played in the New Orleans style.

Junior Raglin was on bass following Jimmy Blanton's death two weeks after the band came to the Panther Room for its July 17 through Aug. 13 engagement.

Ivie Anderson was there and I remember her doing "I Got It Bad," another of my records, with Hodges featured on his hypnotic alto horn. Herb Jeffries sang "Flamingo" and I was impressed by his suave appearance as well as his deep, rich voice.

I recall Webster's solo on "Cottontail," of course. Stewart delighted me with his "Boy Meets Horn," a number I had heard a talented teen-ager play at one of our high school dances.

Juan Tizol, who resembled a banker or doctor, was featured on his own "Caravan." He played a valve trombone, an instrument I hadn't seen. Greer, the drummer, propelled everything in nonchalant fashion from his perch at the rear of the bandstand. Ellington, even more handsome than Jeffries, presided at the keyboard with royal aplomb.

We opted for club sandwiches, rather than "flaming sword" platters. My dad had a bottle of beer and I had a Coke. He enjoyed the show more than I expected, especially the singers and Hodges. But on the way out he said something about never having paid $1.75 for a BLT sandwich before. Back then, the best hamburgers in Burlington sold for a dime. Without, of course, Duke Ellington's band.

My next opportunity to see Ellington was on Sunday night, Jan. 18, 1948, at the Burlington Auditorium. It was bitterly cold and I remember some people leaving at the intermission. The Duke had played some "far out" stuff they didn't care for. If they had stayed they would have enjoyed the medley of popular tunes Ellington wrote.

I was fascinated by the Duke at the piano. It seemed as though he played "Mood Indigo," "Solitude" and "Sophisticated Lady" at the same time. He was still what my jazz buff pals and I liked to refer to as "a suave character."

"Duke Ellington, famed orchestra leader and composer on jazz, the blues and swing tunes, played to a fair-sized audience in Burlington's Memorial Auditorium Sunday night in an ear-splitting concert," The Burlington Hawk-Eye Gazette reported the next day. "His orchestra proved it could swing and has mastered the blues, and the variety won enthusiastic applause. Microphones were in use but they wouldn't have been necessary as the volume would have filled the outdoors."

The brief review mentioned that some of the concert numbers had been played by Ellington in Carnegie Hall. "He swung into popular tunes of his own composition and they were warmly received. The tap-tap-tap of feet could be heard everywhere in the auditorium as spectators tookup the rhythms" it was reported.

"Albert Hibbler, blind singer with a deep baritone voice, was among the favorites of the audience. Kay Davis and Delores Parker, shapely singers, went over well. Johnny Hodges, alto sax, and Ray Nance, trumpet, who doubled on violin and vocal antics, were among the top entertainers. Ellington's distinctive style at the piano kept things rolling."

I remember Ellington saying, as reported in The H-EG, that there were "five great trumpeters and we have all of them." They were, I believe, Shorty Baker, Al Killian, Shelton Hemphill, Francis Williams and Nance.

The trumpeters were featured on a blaring "Trumpet No End," which was a takeoff on "Blue Skies" arranged by Mary Lou Williams.

My highlights also included Nance's violin solos and Hibbler's compelling "I Like the Sunrise." It was the clangor in "Black, Brown and Beige" that turned some of the people off, I believe. Much of it was heavy for me, too.

I saw Ellington at the Chicago Opera House on Feb. 5, 1950. It was a Sunday afternoon and there was a large, cheering crowd.

Tyree Glenn was with the band and I got a kick out of his versatility on vibes and trombone. My most vivid memory is of Glenn, a large man, rushing onto the stage to a fanfare, pushing his vibes with one foot in a cast. He sang, also, making him what football's George Halas would have termed "a triple threat man" with the Bears.

Ellington's band played a one-nighter at the Legion Club in West Point, Ia., on May 14, 1953. I was working the 4 to 12 p.m. shift as an ammo plant safety inspector and missed the event.

After work, I went to a night club to hear a band I enjoyed. On the way home I stopped at an all-night place called Cal's Barbecue where, on weekends, a jazz combo played on a tiny bandstand in the basement.

Paul Gonsalves, who spent the night in town, dropped in around 3 in the morning and I had a great time visiting with him at the bar. He gave me a report on the dance but, unfortunately, did not have his sax with him.

Ellington was en route from West Point, with a night at the Hotel Burlington, to a campus one-nighter at Normal, Ill.

The Burlington paper said the Duke was "in the middle of a tour, mostly one-night stands, that began in New York in late February and would return them to the East Coast by late August. Scheduled for most of June is a three-week appearance at the Blue Note in Chicago."

At West Point, the newspaper noted, Ellington was expected to play such recently-recorded tunes as "Satin Doll" and "Without a Song." Gonsalves told me he played one of my favorite ballads by him, "Laura."

Apr. 9, 1964:

Ellington finally came back to the Burlington area for a one-nighter at Grandinetti's Supper Club in Gulfport, Ill., across the Mississippi from my hometown.

The band, which had begun a tour after returning from a trip to Europe, came to the club around 9:30 p.m. Ellington arrived at 10 o'clock, changed into a grey-checked suit and touched off an awesome number of musical thrills for the 375 people on hand.

"A Train," laid out in relaxed fashion before the Duke came on stage, was sparked by Cat Anderson's subdued trumpet and Jimmy Hamilton's mellow clarinet. Gonsalves played "Laura" to my satisfaction. Ellington, waving to his fans as he nudged his way through the jammed club, got to the piano just as the tenorman ended the tune.

The band returned to its theme. The brash sound of Cootie Williams' open trumpet seemed to slice through the night club's haze. Everyone applauded, realizing the band was getting into high gear.

The Duke, always a great showman, stepped in front of the band, lifted his arms, looked toward the crowd and said: "You're very generous. You're sweet. We love you madly." Somehow, it didn't sound trite.

Back at the piano, Ellington set the tempo for an excerpt from his "Afro-Bossa" LP. The number, also known as "a gut bucket bolero," gave drummer Woodyard a chance to pound away on his skins.

Anderson, likely the best high-note man in jazz, managed to rise above the din with enough altitude to call all the neighborhood's dogs. The crowd loved it.

Hamilton galloped through "Silk Lace," with all the nimbleness of a Goodman or Shaw. Then he picked up the gait on "Honeysuckle Rose," qualifying for the roses.

Famed saxophonist Harry Carney, trombonist Lawrence Brown and clarinetist Russell Procope waxed nostalgic with a medley of "Black and Tan Fantasy," "Creole Love Call" and "The Mooche." The melodies recalled Ellington's impact since the late twenties.

Procope, who had been introduced by Ellington as "a local boy from Des Moines," drew gasps from the crowd as he extended the coda a minute or more. (He was, for the record, born in New York City).

Brown, who played the way most trombonists want to play, departed from his velvet tone for a flurry of jungle-like growls at one point during the medley. Carney, as usual, displayed a vibrant, distinctive tone on his bass clarinet.

The ensemble presented a serious work, "Impressions of the Far East," for, as someone joked, "the first time ever in Gulfport, Illinois." The suite reflected the Duke's genius as a composer and arranger. Particularly his ability to devise tempo changes which, in this case, were accented by an Oriental beat.

"Mood Indigo" and "Satin Doll" sent the supper club's patrons to the dance floor or, in some instances, to the jam-packed bar. I remained in orbit.

There was an interlude to let the musicians refuel. Then the stone-faced Williams, a wizard with mutes and plungers, buzzed his way through a smooth-riding "Caravan." Hodges, the stylish altoist, found his way through the nooks and crannies of "Warm Valley," "All of Me" and "Things Ain't What They Used to Be." Brown made a musical tapestry out of "Poor Butterfly." Carney, on baritone sax, offered "Sophisticated Lady" with an uninterrupted note that exceeded Procope's.

Anderson hit the roof on "Alley Cat." Gonsalves made everyone, including himself, happy with a soft and furry "Sentimental Mood." Then he honked a dozen or more wild choruses on his tour de force "Diminuendo and Crescendo In Blue."

"Harlem," a long number with brassy passages that suggested a rushing subway train, showcased the band's brass. Rolf Ericson, an import from Scandinavia, impressed me with some lush passages on fluegelhorn though Williams was the main soloist.

"Stompin' at the Savoy," a swing era standby, was played at a quicker tempo than on the famous Goodman recording. Hodges drew waves of applause for his "I Let a Song Go Out of My Heart" and "Don't Get Around Much Anymore."

"Hello Dolly," served up in a hurry to answer a request, began in sputtering fashion but became syncopated as Gonsalves found the right groove.

Ellington, who was headed to New York in a few days to record three LP records, had brushed away any thought of retirement during an intermission chat. All he did, the Duke confirmed, was eat, sleep and live music night and day. Especially at night.

"I'll keep going as long as I enjoy it," he remarked. "I don't know why anyone would want to retire unless there was bad health or they got tired of accumulating money. I enjoy what I do. That's all there is to it."

Ellington stressed the importance of his "Symphonic Ellington" LP that was done in 1963 with classical orchestras in Italy, Germany, Sweden and France. "It follows a symphonic kick we began in 1949," he said. "If you're serious about our music it shouldn't be overlooked."

The Duke, an awfully nice man to interview, told me he didn't appreciate having his music pigeonholed as jazz. "It's just music," he declared. "It's what we do. When you get into categories there's bound to be trouble sorting things out."

Ellington was working on three music-based plays. "I have an unlimited accumulation of plans that are impossible," he said. "I sleep whenever I can with the time that's left."

Anderson, the trumpeter, summarized it when he told me: "This isn't just a band. It's an institution."

One sidelight: my sister tested Ellington's well-known smooth touch with women when she was introduced to him at the bar, with a cigarette in one hand and a glass of wine in the other. She spilled some wine on his nifty jacket as she shook his hand, then brushed her cigarette against his sleeve as she wiped the wine away. He shrugged it off with a laugh.

Mar. 22, 1965:

Ellington returned to the club on a Monday night when there was a gap in his itinerary. One of the club's owners told me the band was obtained for, I think, either $1,000 or $1,200. I recall Mercer Ellington, the leader's son and road manager as well as a trumpeter, counting what appeared to be about that much in $100 bills.

The fare was much like 1964, except for some new tunes from "Mary Poppins."

John Lamb's bowed bass gave a jazz lilt to "A Step In Time." Woodyard's cowbells accented a breathless romp through "Supercalifragilisticexpialidocious" as Gonsalves, who was getting to be a habit with me, nearly blew himself into poor health. (I had read that the Duke made it a point to work his ace tenorman especially hard when he had a bad hangover).

I asked Ellington how much of a blow it was in 1940 when Williams left the band to join Benny Goodman. The event was grim enough to prompt Raymond Scott to compose "When Cootie Left the Duke." If it hadn't happened, Ellington responded, "we wouldn't have found Ray Nance."

Nance did a fine job playing "Autumn Leaves" on the violin that night, acting as though nothing had happened when a string broke during his showpiece. He just kept playing, returning in a few minutes to sing, dance and blow his horn. He was, I thought, one of the real individualists in jazz.

Ellington said he was looking forward to the debut of his musical, "Sugar City," for which he had composed 30 tunes. After a trial run in Detroit, he reported, the show would open on Broadway.

Feb. 25, 1971:

The band returned for a sacred music concert on behalf of the St. John AME Church, using the Burlington High School gym.

"His orchestra still swings," I reported in a review for The Hawk Eye. "But the emphasis last night was more on a spiritual message than in the past. It's as though he had a message to get off his chest . . ."

The audience was rather small, around 400. But it was, saxman Norris Turney told me after the concert, "very appreciative."

The program got underway with remarks by the Rev. Robert G. Clay, whose small church brought Ellington to town to help raise money for an activity center. "His music expresses love and joy," Clay noted. "It's music in a contemporary idiom. He was ahead of his time 30 years ago and he's still ahead of his time."

Ellington, wearing a blue satin jacket and a pink shirt, was right on time at 8:15 when the band led off with "Praise God," featuring Carney's authoritative sax. The opener was given some thrust by the nine-member brass section. A promise of things to come.

"Now, Ellington announced, we'll play a selection called 'Supreme Being' with a choir augmenting our orchestra."

Harold Ashby, playing clarinet, did a stalwart job. So did the 20-member local choir led by a tireless civic worker, Cecil Rideout. The singers, with new and difficult chores, handled their assignment with youthful vigor as the band drifted into a rocking groove.

Things began to pop when the Duke introduced his Choirette in a ditty titled "Something About Believing." It was an uptempo number with Gonsalves adding gusto in the right places as the foursome sang.

Devonne Gardner, a talented lyric soprano from Philadelphia, drew praise along with Procope's clarinet on "Almighty God Has His Angels." The blend was reminiscent of early Ellingtonia in the "Mood Indigo" vein.

To me, the evening's instrumental high spot was Williams' plaintive solo on "The Shepherd Who Watches Over the Flock." Cootie, employing a rubber mute and his familiar body gyrations, held the audience spellbound. "His efforts rated a standing ovation," I wrote. "Nothing like the cheers in a BHS basketball game but appreciated nevertheless ."

"Heaven," a bouncer with a Latin beat, featured a choir from the AME church along with some BHS students and

Gardner. Turney, who had replaced Hodges in 1970, proved he was up to the job.

"It's Freedom," a finger-snapper belted out by the Choirette, went on and on uptempo as the singers and band members clapped their hands. Gonsalves, appearing a bit weary that night, was cut off by the Duke just when I thought he was "hitting on all eight."

The Duke, backed by bassist Joe Benjamin, charmed the 400 with a vibrant "Meditation." "This one features our piano player," Ellington had announced.

Mayor Ray Eastin gave Ellington a plaque for his public service after (during the intermission) the leader had changed from his subdued threads into a cream-colored jacket and rose-colored trousers. He thanked the audience for being "so pretty and also so musically mature." Ellington looked good but I had noted during a visit with him at the intermission that he seemed tired and, perhaps, ailing in some way.

Rufus Jones poured it on hot and heavy at the drums on "The Biggest and Busiest Intersection." He got frantic at times. The brass and reed sections returned his fire.

"Too Good to Title," also known as "TGTT," was a wordless musing by Patricia Hoy, a stunning mezzo soprano. The number was dedicated to Jesus Christ who, the Duke reminded, was "the original non-conformist."

Tony Watkins dipped his larynx to the gym's floor on "Don't Get Down On Your Knees Until You've Forgiven Everyone." The leader chipped in with some stride piano as Watkins recited some of the facts of life.

Hoy came back and pulled out all the stops on "Praise God and Dance." Suddenly, there was music everywhere. Ellington's singers were dancing in the aisles. People in the seats were clapping their hands. Gonsalves erupted like a volcano. Several brassmen slammed away on tambourines. The sturdy gym seemed to sway.

Watkins ended the performance with an a capella rendering of "The Lord's Prayer." I drove Turney back to the Holiday Inn where Ellington later played several tunes on a small piano in the cocktail lounge.

Jan. 27, 1974:

Ellington was booked into Pzazz! with his band, but had to cancel the appearance due to his failing health. He died May 24, 1974, at age 75.

My wife and I were in London on Apr. 23, 1988, when Ellington was honored at a concert. I wrote the following review for The Mississippi Rag:

In his book, "Music Is My Mistress," Duke Ellington expressed his fondness, terming it his love, for London.

"It was the first city we went to on the other side of the Atlantic," he wrote, "and in 1933 we could not have had a better stepping stone to Europe."

London re-stated its affection for the late Duke Ellington, with love not too strong a term for it, with an anniversary concert in Queen Elizabeth Hall. He was born Apr. 29 1899.

Queen Elizabeth Hall, a modern theater in South Bank Centre, near Waterloo Bridge, was packed for the event with 2,000 or more Ellington buffs.

Most of the attendees were middle-aged. There were also some teen-agers. I spotted Canadian pianist Oliver Jones, in town for a gig at Pizza On the Park, in the gallery.

The 13-piece Midnight Follies band, led by pianist Keith Nichols and saxman Alan Cohen, focused mostly on vintage Ellingtonia, 1927 to around 1935. It was a brilliant repertory effort as the bandsmen romped through such landmarks as "Birmingham Breakdown," "Stompy Jones" and "Doing the Voom Voom."

Alan Elsdon hit a grandslam when he re-created "Concerto For Cootie," scored by the Duke in 1939 and the closest thing to a current arrangement in the band's book. I was startled when a teen-ager sitting next to me leaped up to applaud the remarkable solo. Millie and I stood, with a bit more reserve, as part of the ovation.

The band, using a banjo and tuba in addition to its more ordinary voicings, played a 1933 chart of "Stormy Weather" in smooth fashion. As the concert went on such departed soloists as Joe Nanton, Freddy Jenkins and Bubber Miley seemed to come back to life.

Adelaide Hall, who recorded "Creole Love Call" with Ellington in 1927, sang two excellent sets. The Brooklyn native was accompanied by pianist Alan Clare. She did several standout numbers, topped by a poignant "Memories of You." Her Ellington numbers included "I Got It Bad" and "It Don't Mean a Thing If It Ain't Got That Swing."

Hall, then 83, was given a huge bouquet and a standing ovation on what would have been Ellington's 89th birthday anniversary, minus a few days.

# Benny Goodman

It was early August, 1942. I was in Chicago with my dad to see some ballgames.

While standing in a sandwich line at Wrigley Field we struck up a conversation with a good-natured black man who was anxious to talk. I told him we were going to see Benny Goodman that night at the Chicago Theater. "Great," he responded. "That man's got rhythm in his bones!"

I squirmed through two movie features that night, hanging on to see Goodman's show a second time. George C. Bied, who had endured Duke Ellington the night before, retired to the Brevoort Hotel on West Madison. I hadn't seen BG before, and only a couple of other big bands. By the time the huge, maroon curtain went up to "Let's Dance" I was high as a kite.

It wasn't Goodman's best band. He had lost Cootie Williams, Sid Catlett, Vido Musso and Georgie Auld one way or another. But he still had Lou McGarity on trombone, Dave Barbour on guitar and, I believe, Hymie Schertzer on alto sax and Jimmy Maxwell on trumpet. It was a long time ago and I didn't take any notes.

Peggy Lee was there, I'm certain. She was the most exciting member of Benny's entourage. Absolutely beautiful to see and to hear.

Down Beat later bemoaned the band's "worried" drummer, Hud Davies, who provided "a terrifically subdued beat" as he "forgot he had other traps than his high hat, upon which he concentrated so thoroughly that he almost fell in."

The journal's "Chicago Band Briefs" pointed out on Sept. 1, 1942, however, that "the guy out front can still play the best clarinet for our money." Benny's piano slot was in flux at the time with Bill Clifton in for audition, then out, and Mel Powell going off to war following duty with Raymond Scott.

Powell was still with the band, as I've remembered it all these years. I'm certain that BG did a peerless job on "Clarinet A La King," just like my Okeh platter, and that the "mediocre" band sounded great. They played "Jersey Bounce" and "String of Pearls" with McGarity and, I think, tenorman Jon Walton getting off sparkling solos. "Mission to Moscow" was kicked off by a flawless trombone choir, unless there was a clinker that has slipped my mind. Schertzer, or whomever, led a smooth as silk sax section through "All I Need Is You" as Lee purred the words.

The next issue of Down Beat included a feature by Mike Levin, who had "a thing" about Goodman in that era, which scorched the King for "slipping" on the clarinet. Benny answered the criticism quite well by going on to excel as a soloist for 44 more years.

I had been a Goodman enthusiast since late 1941 when a schoolmate's older brother played the Sextet's "Good Enough to Keep" and "A Smo-o-o-oth One" on a wind-up phonograph one day at their house. Cootie's trumpet, the riveting Charlie Christian guitar breaks, Auld's driving sax and BG's clarinet hit me like a load of bricks. When I play the original "Smo-o-o-oth One" I still get a boot out of the vocal: "*Mah!*"

I got to buying Goodman records wherever I could find them, getting some of the older Victors by mail from Milt Gabler's Commodore shop in New York. One guy in Texas, who just *had* to have "Body and Soul" by Coleman Hawkins, swapped me a dozen red label Columbias by BG for one new Bluebird by the Hawk. I bought a few combo records, including "Sugar," from George Avakian, who became a well-known jazz critic, while he was still in college. It shocked my father when a COD package arrived with a $8 mint copy of "Clarinetitis" in it. I sold my bicycle and model airplane engine to buy more records. I was hooked.

World War II got in the way of my love affair with jazz, at least as a record collector. There was just one exception. One of my 4-F pals mailed me a copy of the Goodman band's "Darktown Strutter's Ball" while I was at an infantry camp in Texas. They used a record of a bugle call to wake us up, played off a turntable atop the rec hall. I talked a Pfc. into putting my BG record on one morning and, after the reveille, the whole battalion was serenaded by Benny's latest release.

I was home from the ETO in time to be at the Chicago Theater in July, 1945, when the Goodman band shared the bill with "The Affairs of Susan," starring Joan Fontaine and George Brent. The trip to the Windy City and back, something of a thrill itself, was on a gleaming Burlington Route Zephyr.

The Sextet featured bassist Slam Stewart, guitarist Mike Bryan, pianist Charlie Queener, drummer Morey Feld and vibist Red Norvo. I hadn't seen Slam before and was amused by his earnest bowing and humming on "Gotta Be This or That." Trummie Young took some brash solos on trombone, including "Close As Pages In a Book." Dottie Reid, a cute blonde, pitched in with "Paper Moon" and "My Guy's Come Back." I was a guy, I was back. So I imagined she meant me.

"Clarinade," penned for him by Mel Powell, had replaced "Clarinet A La King" as Benny's solo feature.

In 1946, I wrote several notes to Goodman's road manager, Popsie Randolph, asking to be filled in on changes in the band's personnel such trade journals as Variety and Billboard couldn't keep up with. Obviously, I was on a BG binge.

That November, he reported that the roster included drummer Louie Bellson, bassist Harry Babasin, pianist Jess Stacy, guitarist Dale Pierce, vibist Johnny White and vocalist Eve Young. Robert Cutshall was the only trombonist listed and Addison Collins was playing French horn. The trumpeters were Dick Mains, John Best and Nate Kazebier, an Iowan who had been with BG as early as 1935. The saxmen were Clifton Strickland, Larry Mollinelli, John Rotella and Jack Sims, later known as "Zoot."

In 1947, I went straight to the top with a "thank you" note to the King himself, urging him to "keep swinging" and to keep the hot platters coming. "Thank you for your kind note," he replied in a hand-written note on blue stationery.

"We'll certainly keep trying to make the kind of music you like."

This note had some bearing, very likely, on the "summit meeting" I had with BG on July 2, 1948, at the Westchester County Center in White Plains, New York.

I'd written to the Center's manager, telling him it would be nice to meet Goodman when I was in town during a drive to the East Coast with three pals. I looked the manager up when we got there and, to my elation, he rushed me backstage to meet my idol. I was, thoughtfully, fortified by several beers.

Benny was very cordial. We talked for several minutes and he asked if I wasn't the fan who had sent him a photo of a record collection. I had mailed the picture to Goodman's office in 1943 and he remembered my name. I was pleased that he recalled his photo being on top of my record rack in the picture.

Popsie took a photo of me with Benny, and also a shot I asked him to take of tenorman Wardell Gray. He didn't want money for them but he finally accepted $6 for three prints of each shot. I kept Popsie's receipt, scrawled on a scrap of paper, as a souvenir. Popsie was 57 when he died of cancer in 1978. I was surprised to learn that his real name was William Seeznais. Of course it was much easier to be known as "Popsie."

Goodman's combo included clarinetist Stan Hasselgard, pianist Mary Lou Williams, guitarist Billy Bauer, bassist Clyde Lombardi, drummer Mel Zelnick and Gray. Hasselgard was a Swedish whiz who played a lot like BG except for a huskier tone and a penchant for bop. Gray was a prolific bopster with a light touch a la Lester Young. Williams, who looked great that night in a purple gown, played fine piano and had arranged such numbers as "Roll 'Em" for the Goodman band in the thirties.

There were two vocalists, Dolly Houston and Jackie Searle, but most of the fare was instrumental. Williams did "The Man I Love" as her specialty, giving it a light touch of bop.

Gray was featured on "How High the Moon," a mandatory number in most any jazz session in the late forties. Bauer took a ringing solo on "Air Mail Special."

It was a treat to hear Benny and Hasselgard trade choruses on such numbers as "Sweet Georgia Brown" and Barney Kessel's "Swedish Pastry" The group played 23 numbers while I was there, this time with a notebook. The program included such oldies as "Flying Home" and such modern numbers as "Cookin' Up One" and "Mel's Idea," the latter by Powell. I spent the night on Cloud IX.

"The kid does great and Benny's faith in him is well founded," Down Beat reported that summer in appraising Hasselgard. He died in an auto crash on Nov. 23, 1948, at age 26.

Goodman's next career move was a bop-accented big band that featured Gray, who also died young, as well as pianist Buddy Greco, trombonist Eddie Bert, trumpeter Doug Mettome and drummer Sonny Igoe.

The band was booked into the Armar Ballroom near Cedar Rapids, Ia., on Sunday night, Jan. 23, 1949. It snowed so hard that day I could hardly see the highway at times. But I drove 110 miles to the Armar, taking along a teen-ager, Ed Larson, who played drums around Burlington.

It was a shock, to understate it, when we walked into the ballroom and were greeted by a sign in the lobby, with Goodman's picture on it, saying he wasn't with the band "due to illness." (Russ Connor's latest Goodman discography notes that BG had missed some performances in New York due to "severe bronchitis" and stayed home to recuperate as the band went to the West Coast on an extended tour).

It was a fine band playing such modern charts as Chico O'Farrell's "Undercurrent Blues," which I considered to be in the middle between swing and bop. It featured a driving solo by Gray and a lift from Igoe's drums. Some of the old tunes such as "Don't Be That Way" sounded as they always had except for some bop flourishes that did no harm.

But none of it sounded right without BG's clarinet. The void was filled, about as well as possible, with some very tasteful muted trumpet solos by Mettome. It looked odd but was probably a better device than trying to expect one of the sidemen to play Benny's part on clarinet.

It was a long drive home, including the possibility of getting lost, but we stayed until past midnight to get our money's worth. Greco was impressive at the piano and Igoe gave my young companion something to think about. The ensemble was very relaxed, a condition that could have been attributed to Benny's absence, I suppose.

Terry Swope, a statuesque blonde who had sung with Bob Strong and Buddy Rich, was a real eyeful. I remember her doing a nice job on "Lover Man" and being joined by a group called the Clarinaders on "Am I Blue?" Greco, a very able vocalist himself, did "Having a Wonderful Wish" and a boppish "Ooo-Bla-Dee."

I lost some interest in jazz, except for playing my records, during a 20-year span when, to my knowledge, the King of Swing didn't perform nearby in Iowa or Illinois. I also had some personal distractions that contributed to my ennui with respect to music.

Sept. 2, 1972:

My spirit was rekindled when Goodman brought a top-drawer combo to Iowa State University at Ames. There was a near-capacity crowd of 10,000 in the mammoth Hilton Coliseum when, in an unusual role for him, Benny played "warm up" for Andre Kostelanetz and the New York Philharmonic.

I saw Goodman at the Ramada Inn a few hours before the concert, learning that he had Derek Smith on piano and George Duvivier on bass. Bobby Rosengarden played drums, hobbling on and off stage with one foot in a cast. Bucky Pizzarelli played guitar and Peter Appleyard was on vibes. Urbie Green was the group's sure-toned trombonist.

The combo played standard Goodman fare. I never tired of hearing "Avalon," "Poor Butterfly," "After You've Gone" and "Memories of You." Most of the audience would have felt short-changed, I'm sure, if the group hadn't played music they recognized.

I had to sit behind the band that night, unable to get a good look at the faces of Benny and the others as they played to the better seats. "If it had been Miles Davis," my friend Ralph Drish noted, "you would have had one of the best seats in the house."

Goodman's portion of the concert rated lavish coverage in The Des Moines Register. "It is an aristocratic, full sound that he has in complete control at all times," reviewer Nick Baldwin wrote, "and (Goodman's) phrasing is embellished by a variety of subtle ornamentations."

In a sidebar story, the paper reported that Benny was "delighted" to learn that his motel had an indoor pool. "In his well-cut suit, conservative tie and neatly trimmed hair, he would blend in perfectly at any gathering of bankers or at a board meeting."

I recall that BG was wearing a nifty seersucker jacket when he left the Ramada in a bigwig's Mercedes to go to the coliseum. "Anything goes today," he'd remarked when a man in an eye-jarring jacket walked through the motel's lobby.

Jim Dougherty, a jazz broadcaster at Iowa City, was among those impressed by the caliber of the combo Goodman brought to Iowa City's Hancher Auditorium on Dec. 5-6, 1974. It was to have been a one-nighter but a second concert was added to satisfy the demand for tickets.

Dougherty, who'd anticipated a lesser group to come to the hinterlands, found out that the roster would include pianist Hank Jones, bassist Stewart, tenor saxman Al Klink, trumpeter Marvin Stamm, trombonist Mickey Gravine, Pizzarelli and Rosengarden.

I went to both concerts, of course. The rhythm section opened each night, without Goodman, doing such numbers as "Tangerine," "Satin Doll" and an Ellington medley.

The first night, Goodman kicked off with "I Want To Be Happy" and then slowed the tempo for "Here, There and Everywhere" and a gorgeous "Yesterday." Klink was featured on "Girl From Impamena," Gravine did "That's All" and Stamm soloed on "I Love You," with a modern touch.

Pizzarelli played a reflective "Mirage" and the group romped through "Slipped Disc" and, to the audience's immense approval, "The Entertainer," with Benny cutting up like a roaring twenties ragtimer.

It was more of the same the next night plus an elegant feature by Jones, Ray Noble's "The Very Thought of You," and an enjoyable "Play Fiddle Play" by Slam. "Memories of You" and "Runnin' Wild" were added while "Lady Be Good" and "After You've Gone" were dropped.

I wasn't sure if I could see Benny or not, so I mailed a copy of Popsie's 1948 photo for him to sign. It got lost in the mail a few weeks but finally arrived along with a note from BG referring to it as "a good picture." He autographed it with his "very best wishes."

Goodman was available, it turned out, and my wife got some nice photos of us visiting in the dressing room.

July 4, 1976:

We drove to Ravinia Park, north of Chicago, to see a Goodman combo that included pianist Tommy Fay, bassist Mike Moore, guitarist Gene Bertoncini, drummer Connie Kay, tenorman Buddy Tate, cornetist Warren Vaché and vibist Appleyard.

It was a superb group which Goodman went out of his way to praise for its marvelous sound. He opened with a brisk "Chicago" and then dedicated a delicate "Dearly Beloved" to Bobby Hackett and Johnny Mercer.

Vaché did a warm solo on "You Took Advantage of Me," recalling Bix. Moore contributed a playing of "Come Sunday" that would have sounded right on a symphony stage, though it was jazz. Benny played a Sondheim tune, "Have You Met My Wife?", I hadn't heard him do. Tate delivered a suspenseful, gutty solo on "Sing, Sing, Sing." The combo tore "Indiana," "I Found a New Baby" and "After You've Gone" limb from limb, leaving enough bones for Appleyard to do "Gone" as his dazzling encore.

Goodman played extremely well all night and shared the spotlight with his sidemen. What, I wondered, motivated people to accuse him of being too self-centered to feature the musicians in his employ?

Kay was "discreetly unobtrusive" throughout the night, reviewer John McDonough noted in Down Beat, "except for a powerful display on 'Sing, Sing, Sing.'"

Expanding his format without having to hire a bus, Goodman delivered himself and his clarinet to Elgin, Ill., on Nov. 21, 1976, for a concert with the Elgin Symphony Orchestra. It happened to be my birthday and my sister-in-law, Martha Irish, obtained front row seats.

The program ranged from Benny playing a von Weber concertina with the symphony to a Peter Knight medley that included "Here's That Rainy Day," "I've Got You Under My Skin," "Honeysuckle Rose," "Send In the Clowns" and "Goodbye." I especially enjoyed the way "Rose" was done first as a ballad and then uptempo.

I talked to Benny during the intermission, asking him for an interview in two weeks at Davenport. "I'll be there," he promised.

It was the same program with the Quad-City Symphony on Dec. 5, 1976, with an apology from Goodman for not bringing his jazz combo along. To atone, he played a chorus of "Avalon," with no accompaniment, and then "I'm Coming Virginia" as a tribute to Bix.

Iowa's cold weather might have been a shock to Goodman as he stepped from the steam heat in Davenport's Masonic Temple onto the ice-coated alley behind the building. He had flown up from the Caribbean for the three symphony concerts. We waited as the symphony manager, Lance Willett, got his car to drive Benny, with me in the back seat, to the airport for the 6:14 p.m. flight to New York.

BG looked imposing, in a tan topcoat and a cerulean scarf, and a teen-ager asked me if he was with the CIA? "No," I said. "He's a BG."

There wasn't time for autographs, only for some of the musicians to shake Benny's hand. He had paused only to change shirts and have a highball in his dressing room.

We stopped a few minutes at the Clayton House and Willett went in for Goodman's bags. It was chilly in the car and the aging virtuoso, then 67, was irked that the car's engine had been turned off, robbing him of warmth from the heater.

I asked about his recent tour of Eastern Europe, that hadn't received much mention in the papers. He told me the combo included drummer Barrett Deems, pianist John Bunch, Vaché and Tate. He couldn't remember the name of the guitar player, who turned out to be Cal Collins. I said something about Tate, recalling his stellar performance at Ravinia, and was pleased when Goodman asked what I thought of his work.

"The bad weather kept some of them away" Goodman said in explaining why some seats were empty at the just-ended concert. All the seats had been sold, Willett assured him.

Amid some yawns, Goodman talked about a Mozart piece he had recorded with the BBC orchestra during his recent tour. He also mentioned a jazz date the next weekend at Stamford, Conn., where he lived. "I hope they'll send me a tape from BBC," he said, "and also one from this weekend."

"No," Goodman blurted when I asked if he had any plan to form a big band. "We'd have to play every night to make it pay and that's too much."

"Sure," he replied when I asked if he planned to keep playing rather than, perhaps, retire to his home on St. Maarten. "I don't plan to do anything else."

Fishing for more small talk, I brought up the subject of the mid-thirties incident in Iowa when his band's bus ran over a case holding two new trumpets belonging to Harry James.

"It didn't happen at Marshalltown," he snapped. "It was at Oelwein."

Goodman laughed a bit later, after another yawn, when something reminded him of the Ted Weems dance band. "There isn't any Ted Weems anymore," he mused. "Only a ghost band. What'd he used to play? I can't remember."

"I think it was 'Heartaches,'" I said, as the talk got smaller. "Perry Como sang with him and somebody whistled."

"You're doing good down there," he said when I told him we'd had Armstrong, Kenton, Herman and Al Hirt at our Steamboat Days. I wanted to book Goodman but had been told by his secretary, Muriel Zuckerman, that Benny wasn't doing festivals.

I congratulated him on winning the 1976 Down Beat poll for clarinetists. "Oh," he said. "Did I win that?"

At the airport, Willett and I carried Goodman's bags into the terminal. He carried his clarinet and also a red, white and blue bag full of stuff from the Caribbean.

He got in line, apparently unrecognized by the others headed to the 727 jet to Chicago and then Kennedy Airport. "Thanks Dan," he said, then waved before disappearing into the crowd.

I was at the Civic Opera House in Chicago on Feb. 19, 1977, when the Goodman Sextet played a benefit for the Sager Solomon Schechter Day School. The group included Percy Heath on bass along with Bunch, Kay, Tate, Collins and Vaché.

It was in this era, I think, when McDonough made some references to Goodman's "Rolls Royce rhythm section" with Bunch, Collins, Kay and such bassists as Moore, Stewart, Heath and Major Holley in it. Also, bassist Phil Flanigan and, at times, drummer Chuck Riggs and guitarist Pizzarelli.

My small tape recorder picked up highlights of the Opera House program. "Body and Soul" was an unusual duet by Collins, who 'played beautifully, and BG. Heath showed off a throbbing beat on "Lady Be Good" as Benny impressed me with a low register solo.

Oct. 29, 1977:

Susie Melikian, a young East Coast singer, added some sex appeal as Bunch, Vaché, Tate, Collins, Kay and Moore accompanied Goodman at the C.Y. Stephens Auditorium in Ames. The attractive theater, with superb acoustics, seemed to invigorate the mostly-familiar program.

"Girl Friend," by Rodgers & Hart, was a peppy addition to the repertoire. Melikian sang "Gee Baby Ain't I Good to You" and "Love Me or Leave Me." The combo played "Have You Met Miss Jones?" and Vaché delivered an uncluttered, deep-toned solo on "I Thought About You" that was a jewel,

The same group, except for Stewart on bass, Wayne Andre on trombone and Debi Craig doing the vocals, appeared at Powell Symphony Hall in St. Louis on Mar. 11, 1978.

BG played a barnburner solo on "Lady Be Good," almost entirely different than at Chicago, that was so full of squeaks, squawks and slurs it reminded me of Pee Wee Russell. This, I think, was what Deems had in mind when he told me Goodman played "more in one night than I ever heard Armstrong play in years."

We had coffee with Benny at the Chase Hotel after the concert. I appreciated how nice he was to Millie and got him to autograph a new book of mine that included the interview I'd done en route to the Moline Airport. He asked if I "made out all right" on the book. I'll never know how he'd have reacted if I had denied making a profit.

I congratulated Goodman on the LP set from his Carnegie Hall Concert in 1978, that was panned by many of the critics. It was mostly a party, I figured, and not meant to be a re-creation of Jan. 16, 1938. He beamed when I singled out the full band's silken rendition of "Stardust." "Yeah," he remarked, with some pride. "You know who arranged that? It was Gordon Jenkins."

We went back to Ames on June 1, 1979, for a concert that featured trombonist Jack Gail, drummer Ron Davis, Bunch, Stewart, Vaché, Klink and Bertoncini. The SRO crowd jumped up with applause before Goodman played a note. He responded with a fast "I Want to Be Happy," a velvety "Send In the Clowns" and a smoldering "Avalon."

Goodman was the star at the first annual Chicago Jazz Festival on Sunday night, Sept. 2, 1979, and reportedly donated his fee to charity.

The combo included Bunch, Kay, Moore and Bertoncini. Polly Podewell sang "Devil and the Deep Blue Sea" and the group, paced by an enthused BG attired in a navy blue jacket and white pants, sailed through ten of his standards.

Mel Torme, also a Windy City native, joined Benny for a set that gave Mel an opportunity to pound out "Sing, Sing, Sing" at the drums Gene Krupa played at Carnegie Hall in 1938. The crowd in Grant Park ate it up. Torme did a set with a Chicago-based big band that included "Ridin' High" and "When the Sun Comes Out." It was the first I had seen him since 1942. He had changed.

July 12, 1980:

Goodman was booked for a concert at the Des Moines Civic Center, which we planned to attend. It was cancelled, though, along with 11 other appearances when he developed back problems. Back pains had, of course, plagued BG for more than 40 years and were, I have heard, a likely reason for his irascibility.

It was a dilemma for the new theater, which was trying to build a reputation with top-drawer attractions. Some 1,100 tickets had been sold and Gerald Bloomquist, the theater manager, asked Goodman to refund $2,100 for its expenses.

"He was very much a gentleman about it'" Bloomquist said when the payment was made. "It was a whale of a nice gesture on his part," a theater trustee added. "He didn't have to do it."

The last Goodman performance I attended was at Ames on Apr. 16, 1983. Trumpeter Spanky Davis and trombonist Joel Helleny comprised what BG introduced as "our heavy artillery." But the combo's most unusual feature, more so than Davis' girth, was the presence of three guitar players: Chris Flory, Bucky Pizzarelli and his son, John.

Bucky and John played a medley of "Autumn Leaves" and "Autumn In New York." They also did a nimble "In the Dark," by Beiderbecke, and a contemporary "I'm Hip." Mike LeDonne, the pianist was featured on "Gone With the Wind." The guitar players merged for a soft, memorable "Mirage."

June 13, 1986:

Millie phoned me at work to tell me Goodman had died. It wasn't like losing a family member or a close friend. But it was painful news and it made me feel numb.

I wanted to do something. So I went to a local radio station, KBUR, and talked on the air about how much Benny had done to popularize jazz, to aid racial integration and to entertain the troops in the forties. I compared his impact on musical trends with that of Elvis Presley and the Beatles. "Goodman's success helped the entire music business," I explained. "People turned from Mickey Mouse bands to swing."

The Des Moines Register recalled the "gentlemanly" way Goodman had helped the Civic Center. An editorial lamented that his death had "reduced the already slim field of musical big names capable of drawing crowds."

The Chicago Tribune editorialized that BG could "do anything with a clarinet except make it sound bad," adding that his secret was simple enough: "He concentrated on being a musician rather than being a star."

The Sunday Advocate, which was Benny's hometown paper in Connecticut, remembered him as: "The quiet guy who lived down the block. The one with the horn-rimmed glasses who always walked alongside that funny dog he loved so much. A consummate host friends would ring in the New Year with at his North Stamford home."

His medium-size house was unpretentious, the paper added. "Its walls, shelves and bureaus are filled with photos, artwork, mementos and music. There's an extensive garden where Goodman liked to walk through a lush carpet of green grass to see if there were blueberries or raspberries to be picked. And there is a swimming pool. The house was perfect for privacy, something Goodman jealously guarded."

The Sunday Advocate reminded that Goodman "shattered the racial barrier in the band business by being the first leader of a major white orchestra to hire black musicians. Pianist Teddy Wilson and vibraphonist Lionel Hampton."

I wrote an op-ed page article for The Des Moines Register that recalled the one-nighter Goodman's band played at Oelwein, Ia., in 1937. The bus actually did run over HJ's trumpets at Marshalltown, I concluded, quoting what the Goodman book, "Kingdom of Swing," seemed to say about the disaster's locale.

Goodman might have been mixed up about where it was the bus "flattened the trumpets like a sheet of music." More important, I pointed out, "he was a genius as a clarinetist and bandleader, and a fine man."

Since 1986, such jazzmen as drummers Louie Bellson and Don Lamond have told me how much they respected Goodman.

"He was tight with money because of being raised in the ghetto," Bellson said. "Stan Getz and I agreed on that. I think he was entitled to some eccentricities. He taught me much of what I had to know to get where I am in music."

Lamond stuck up for Benny when some of the panelists at the Woody Herman reunion in September, 1993, took some cheap shots at him. "He had a lot of respect for the Woody Herman band," Lamond pointed out. "The guy was a genius. Don't forget that."

"I liked him," Doc Cheatham told me when I asked about his experiences playing with Goodman. Dan Barrett, a trombonist with Benny in the eighties, said it was often "their own fault" when musicians had ongoing problems with BG.

I wrote an article for The Mississippi Rag to debunk some of the misconceptions about Goodman over the years. Regarding comments about Goodman's alleged jealousy, I wrote: "I do not recall Harry James, Lionel Hampton, Teddy Wilson,. Ziggy Elman, Jess Stacy and Gene Krupa, who became nearly as famous as Goodman himself, being hidden backstage. Nor do I recall other bandleaders devoting entire records to sidemen as Benny did for Charlie Christian on "Solo Flight" and Chris Griffin on 'Boy Meets Horn.'"

Also, I don't remember Tommy Dorsey featuring another trombonist or Harry James a trumpeter the way Goodman put Hasselgard in the spotlight with his clarinet.

It is a lie when people say Goodman did not acknowledge the contributions of the Henderson arrangements to his band's success. He actually cited Fletcher's importance many times and, in fact, dedicated his final TV show to Henderson in March, 1986.

Buddy DeFranco once told me that Goodman was "a businessman first of all, then a musician." I don't think he meant that as a slight to BG's musicianship or a criticism of his ability to make money. Henderson went broke being lax on discipline, after all. It appears Goodman learned something from Fletcher's bad experience.

I've read that Goodman gave money to Bunny Berigan's widow and to Eddie Sauter's wife when Sauter was ill. He gave generously to the Hull House, according to newspaper reports, and to other charities.

Marian McPartland termed Benny "a warm human being" in an article she wrote for Down Beat in 1964. "Basically, he's a simple man, with no ostentation and very honest."

I wrote to Benny's daughter, Rachel Edelson, in 1988 when I heard she was collecting memorabilia for a tribute to him. I offered a few pictures, including one of him playing trumpet on a theater stage. I'd been told the picture wasn't too unusual but she had never seen it.

When she replied she admitted that Goodman had shown "a kind of indifference, at times, to some of the concerns that keep the world turning smoothly." She said she had "long struggled to get the many sides of him sorted out in my own mind."

He was usually wrapped up in his music and I'm thankful for that. He left politics to the politicians.

I also appreciate that he treated me so well. He might have thought I had some importance in show business, which I didn't. Maybe he just appreciated my taste in clarinet players or the fact that I never got in his hair. All I wanted from him was music and a few comments over the years.

# BG's Tributes

Walt Levinsky's American Jazz Orchestra did such a great job playing the music of Benny Goodman my wife and I went to Michael's Pub four nights in a row in July, 1987.

Michael's Pub, at 211 East 55th Street in New York, proved to be an ideal venue for recapturing the Goodman sound. The sound system is excellent and we managed to be close enough to the bandstand for an intimate view of the 14 musicians and the attractive vocalist, Lynn Roberts, who sang well and had to be older than she appeared.

It was a kick to hear the durable Goodman charts again, including Mel Powell's "Clarinade" and Eddie Sauter's "Benny Rides Again." Levinsky, a real pro, romped through the uptempo "Clarinade" in grand fashion, nearly as fluidly as Benny himself. But it's a tough number to play night after night, he pointed out. "I wish Benny had paid Mel more money," he quipped. "If he had maybe Mel wouldn't have written pieces that are so hard to play."

"Benny Rides Again," which was an update of "Sing, Sing, Sing" in some ways, must be awfully hard to play with its complex, subtle changes. The Levinsky band did it very well, the way Sauter wrote it when BG reassembled his band after being sidelined by a bad back in 1940. Levinsky's version had the lilt the number had when played by the Goodman crew, with Harry Jaeger on drums. In this case it was Butch Miles driving the rhythm section each night as the band played the Sauter score and then Jimmy Mundy's "Sing, Sing, Sing" as a double-barreled treat. Of the two, "Sing, Sing, Sing" generates more power while "Benny Rides Again" implies its subtle drive.

Levinsky was proud enough of his band to list the names of all the sideman on a signboard in front of the Pub, a thoughtful touch. Marty Napoleon was at the piano. The saxmen included tenorman Babe Clark, whose solo on "Sing, Sing, Sing" was authentic to the 1938 approach.

Urbie Green and Eddie Bert rated solo spots on the trombone. Spanky Davis, Randy Sandke and Warren Vache divided solo honors on trumpet, with Spanky a tower of power on "And the Angels Sing."

It was advertised that all the bandsmen had played with Goodman. I didn't recall Napoleon and a few others being with Benny, but they may have been with him briefly. The band was very well rehearsed and played the Fletcher Henderson numbers, including "King Porter Stomp" and "Down South Camp Meeting," with consummate ease. One of the trumpeters did fluff a note on "King Porter," come to think of it. That probably happened during Goodman's hey-day.

Vache' and Green were spotlighted on "Oh Baby," which was more casual, and a bit more loose, than it was when it was released as a 12-incher around 1946. The arrangement used by Levinsky seemed to be more sketchy than the original, an invitation for improvisation that doesn't always come off as intended.

Roberts, who had been with Goodman in 1961, was up to the occasion doing Helen Forrest's "More Than You Know," from the Sauter arrangement, and Peggy Lee's "Why Don't You Do Right?" She captured Lee's clipped, off-hand style very well and approached Forrest's range.

Levinsky, who was with Goodman in the mid-fifties, is no King of Swing with the clarinet, a fact he alluded to on stage. But he is "not chopped liver," as the saying goes, with the licorice stick. He was at his best, I thought, on the slower numbers. "Memories of You," played tenderly with just the rhythm section, came very close to BG himself.

After one of his shows, I made it a point to compliment Vachc' by telling him how much Goodman thought of his playing. He was, in fact, the only young musician Benny singled out for praise when I interviewed him on the way to Moline, Ill.

"Such bands have been put together in the past for nostalgic purposes," it was noted by John S. Wilson in The New York Times, "but they have rarely been heard in performances so crisply authoritative." The band was so good, in my opinion, it deserves more exposure than a few night club dates and an occasional festival.

In the spring of 1991, the Levinsky band played a tribute to Goodman as a highlight of the 11th annual Sarasota Jazz Festival. The event was, appropriately, dedicated to Hal Davis, who founded the Sarasota Jazz Club and had worked as Goodman's road manager and publicist.

It was pretty much the same band we had seen in New York, except for the inspired addition of Peter Appleyard on vibes. He played a supercharged "Fascinating Rhythm" and joined with Napoleon at the piano to tear things up a bit on "After You've Gone."

Joe Wilder delivered some punch with his trumpet solo on "Roll 'Em" in a chart updated from the thirties. "Benny Rides Again" was a big hit. The band played "Memories of You" as a tribute to Al Klink, who was going to play at the festival but died a few weeks before it was held. I recalled the night in Iowa City when BG introduced Klink as "my old friend."

Clark was on hand with his tenor to put some sock into the second part of "Sing, Sing, Sing." The number triggered an ovation from the crowd in Van Wezel Hall. (Van Wezel is a beautiful concert hall but the exterior always reminds me of a purple souffle).

There was a memorable touch when Milt Hinton, the veteran bassist, was honored for his many contributions to jazz. Milt seems to be at nearly every jazzfest we attend. So it was no surprise when he and Mona were the first people Millie and I recognized in the lobby at the Hyatt.

Sept. 2, 1988:

The Chicago Jazz Festival honored Goodman with a first-class band assembled by Bob Wilber that had some of the spectators dancing in the aisles. Much like the Paramount Theater, circa 1937.

It was a precise band, attired in tuxes, that put an authentic-sounding imprint on the music BG rode to fame with in the swing era. Wilber is a facile perfectionist in the Goodman tradition, who swings. His band included a number of sidemen who played for BG in his later years.

I especially enjoyed the Wilber outfit's treatment of "Roll 'Em," done at a faster pace than the original version with an extended boogie solo on piano. "Bugle Call Rag" was driven by what BG liked to refer to as "that old pepper." "Sing, Sing, Sing" was a faithful re-creation except that no one can duplicate Harry James.

Mar. 12, 1992:

Peanuts Hucko and an "alumni" orchestra played a salute to Goodman at Augustana College in Rock Island, Ill., with a young group that seemed to have little if any connection to the swing era except for their enthusiasm.

Hucko, an excellent clarinetist, played with Goodman and his wife, Louise Tobin, sang with BG aroung 1939-40. Buddy Greco, also featured in the program, has done well as a vocal stylist since the era of BG's bop band.

The band played such favorites as "Jersey Bounce" and "Benny Rides Again" from arrangements that tended to be more simple than the originals, though I doubt if that made them easy to play.

Tobin sang well on "The Man I Love." Greco, much more polished than in 1949, played a sonata-like piano solo on "Misty" that Erroll Garner probably would have loved. He also did a Nat Cole medley that made me want to hear more.

Oct. 21 1993:

Carnegie Hall was the launching pad when the house jazz band, led by Jon Faddis, fused the past with the present, and perhaps the future, in a concert of Goodman's music.

"Where other repertory groups might change the emphasis in an interpretation or open up solo space beyond the constraints of the original three-minute recording of a piece," reviewer Peter Watrous noted in The New York Times, "the Carnegie Hall band radically rewrote the material."

He added: "The band, tight and precise, swung hard. But its most important accomplishment of the evening was to start an essential process: the reworking of original source material, with no sense of restraint."

That could be dangerous , I fear.

# Count Basie

"Man, " said Count Basie. "You really know how to satisfy!"

He was thanking me for a pack of Chesterfields I gave him as we sat down for an interview in the lobby of the Hotel Burlington. It was mid-afternoon but the tobacco counter was closed for some reason. Basie, who had just gotten out of bed, was having a nicotine fit and I suddenly found myself with an opportunity to do a favor for a musician I'd admired since 1942.

It was May 8, 1959. It had been a dull news day and, around 2 p.m., I was ready to knock off and go get a beer. But someone at the hotel phoned with a news tip telling us that Basie and his band had spent the night there on their way to Fairfield. The destination was Parsons College, for the "Spring Fling'" in a town too small for a hotel that could hold a busload of musicians.

One of my pals, Bob Wilson, grabbed a Speed Graphic and went to the hotel. One of the Count's aides went to the house phone, called his boss and in a few minutes we were on a sofa and ready to talk about jazz.

The interview, including some preliminaries, lasted about 20 minutes. It was printed in The Burlington Hawk Eye on May 12, 1959, and went about like this:

Count Basie, who has delighted millions with his keyboard pyrotechnics since hitting the swing band road to fame in 1936, played to an audience of one last week.

The attentive listener and curious question man was a jazz addict named Bied, who has been a Basie fan since he plunked down a half-dollar for a copy of the Count's "Swinging at the Daisy Chain."

As is often the case with people overflowing with talent and fame, Basie proved to be cooperative, humble and just a bit absentminded.

Q - Where have you been playing? Where are you going to play next?

A - "We've been on the West Coast and we'll be going back to New York to play at Birdland and then at the Waldorf-Astoria. How's that for a jump, Birdland to the Waldorf?"

Q - Where were you last night?

A - "Let me see. Oh hell, I can't remember. I'll have to ask someone. Hey, where'd we play last night?" ("It was Canton, Missouri," the man who had phoned Basie's room yelled back).

Q - You've been in the music business 20 or 30 years now. Do you enjoy it as much as you used to?

A - "Oh yes, definitely. I certainly get as big a kick out of it now. Outside of the fact that it pays my rent, I'm in this business because I enjoy it. It's not a drag."

Q - Who's featured in the band these days?

A - "That's a strange thing. Actually, everybody's featured in our band. Joe Newman, Frank Foster. They're all soloists. They're all part of the band and that's a fine deal for everyone."

Q - What do you think about some of the younger bands that are on their way up?

A - "Well, I really don't have too much of a chance to hear them, unfortunately. But I'm very interested in the kids (Basie was born in 1904) and I'm glad to see them getting along. That's what we need. It helps develop good values for the teen-agers."

Q - What do you think of rock 'n roll?

A - "I think it stands for something. The beat got the kids to dancing. But of course anything can exaggerated . . . overdone, I mean."

Q - Do the music fans still crowd around the bandstand the way they did in swing era?

A - "They do, and it's very pleasing to us. An odd thing happened a while back the West Coast. We were playing a Sunday dance and everyone pulled their chairs onto the dance floor and just sat and listened. It was one hell of a tribute to the band. The young people understand what we're doing. Maybe it's on the square side for them, but they're trying to dig it. After all, we're playing the kind of music their parents, their uncles and their aunts used to listen and dance to."

Q - Do you trade arrangements with other bands?

A - "Yes, we do. We have an arrangement of my pet tune, 'I've Got My Love To Keep Me Warm.' from Les Brown. But you know, it just doesn't sound right when we play it. Les has a fine band. I've called it my band the past 15 years."

Q - What do you do with yourself when you aren't on the road with your band?

A - "I like to go to movies, mostly Westerns. I'm a baseball fan and I enjoy going to the race track. I have a little cocktail lounge in New York and get a kick out of tending bar there when I'm around town."

Q - Who do you pull for in baseball?

A - "The Yankees, of course."

Q - Aren't you concerned about them so far this season?

A - "Naw. They're just losing to make it interesting. So more people will go to the ballparks."

Count Basie's first one-nighter in Burlington had been in December, 1940. He was booked into Memorial Auditorium by a friend of mine, the late Sam Brooks. Sam, who was in his early twenties at the time, had a dance band that traveled around in Packard limos with his name on the side of them. He hoped to gain some regional recognition but the band broke up when an agent in Chicago suggested that someone with drawing power, perhaps Charlie Teagarden, should front it. This would have taken Sam out of the picture. The band was dissolved when he went into service.

"Having Basie for a dance was a labor of love," Sam told me around 1980. "I asked a classmate, Clyde White, to help me by telling his black friends about the dance. He got in touch with jazz fans as far as 200 miles away. Some of them came from Des Moines and other far-away points."

Brooks charged $2 per couple for blacks to dance and 55 cents for whites to sit in the balcony. "The balcony seats were sold out," he recalled. "During all the excitement it was hard to keep the spectators from spilling onto the dance floor. The Count and his men were in top form. In those days we called it swing."

Brooks reported that Basie carried three trumpeters, three trombonists, five saxophonists and a four-man rhythm section, including himself. Walter Page was on bass, Jo Jones was at the drums and Freddie Green, who stayed with Basie until the end, was the guitarist.

Al Killian, known as a high-note man, led a trumpet section that included Harry Edison and Buck Clayton. Dickie Wells, Vic Dickenson and Dan Minor were the trombonists. Tab Smith and Earle Warren played alto sax. Buddy Tate and Don Byas played tenors and Jack Washington played baritone sax.

"Basie carried two vocalist," Brooks related. "Helen Humes, who sang ballads and blues, and the great Jimmy Rushing, who was known for his 'Harvard Blues' and 'Outskirts of Town,' were both in Burlington that night. Helen Humes was always very much underrated."

Basie was " particularly delighted" with the auditorium's piano. "It was a Baldwin concert grand," Sam reported, "that had been custom made for Jose Iturbi who played it when the auditorium was dedicated." (The piano, built in 1936, was still in use as this book went to press).

In 1940, the Basie band's fee was $650. It was a mid-week event and tab could have been as much as $1,000 for a one-nighter on a weekend. "Black bands and many white bands had to struggle to make ends meet," Sam remarked. "The Basie band didn't really establish a comfortable situation until years later when Sinatra and Tony Bennett helped the Count break into Las Vegas scene."

July 11, 1947:

The first time I had seen Basie's band was at the Paradise Club, which resembled a prohibition era roadhouse, at 220 North Illinois Avenue in Atlantic City. It was a dark room, with a low ceiling and small tables surrounding a stage and dance floor. Everything was bathed in white, amber, yellow and blue spotlights during the show.

The club's waiters were well-attired, though it wasn't a posh sort of place. There was a camera girl, showing off nifty legs in a short skirt, taking souvenir photos with a big, heavy Speed Graphic.

The floor show featured two black comedians, Stump and Stumpy. Their routine included a zany satire on "Duel In the Sun," a popular movie, in which one of them whipped out a water pistol and shot his partner between the eyes. Their act was a howl, with my pal and I lubricated with drinks from the bar.

I did, however, think well enough to jot down the names of the band members, provided by Basie's road manager. Edison, Wells, Tate, Washington, Green and Page were there. So were trumpeters Snooky Young, Emmett Berry and Ed Lewis; trombonists Ted Donnelly, Bill Johnson and George Matthews; altoists Charlie Price and Preston Love; tenorman Paul Gonsalves; and drummer Jimmy Crawford, who had propelled Jimmie Lunceford's great band from 1928 to 1943 and was "sitting in" briefly with Basie.

There were three vocalist. Rushing performed such standards of his as "Harvard Blues" and "Jimmy's Blues," a number featuring the robust trombone of Matthews. Bob Bailey crooned "Danny Boy" during the floor show. Ann Baker was featured on "Meet Me At No Special Place," one of Basie's more popular RCA discs at that time.

Other numbers played by the impeccable, swinging band that night included "Rose Room," "Mutton Leg," "South," "Free Eats," "Basie Boogie," "Swinging the Blues," "Bill's

Mill," " Jalousie" and an opus called "Paradise Squat" that was, I figured, named in honor of the club.

I recall Gonsalves doing a long, scorching solo on "Mutton Leg" and a group from the band singing "Free Eats," a tune I had on a 78-rpm disc. "Jalousie" was the same arrangement played by Harry James and it was done note for note as the Music Makers did it, with Edison doing the trumpet solo.

In 1948, the Basie band was booked into the National Guard Armory at Hannibal, Mo., about 100 miles south of Burlington. My pal from the Atlantic City trip, Dawson Brown, went with me. It was a tough drive back and we finally got home around 3 in the morning.

Dawson was "between jobs" at the time and I surely skipped a couple of a.m. classes at the junior college the next day. I remember Basie playing mostly jump tunes. The crowd was noisy and large. Gonsalves was still with the band and made the air blue, per his custom, with his solos. The stone-walled armory was an odd place for a one-nighter but the chemistry worked.

My next chance to see Basie was at Parsons College in Fairfield, Ia., around the spring of 1962. The public was allowed to attend the concert in the school's fieldhouse.

"Lil Darlin'" was Basie's most popular tune at that time, played gently with a quiet beat. Wess was in the spotlight much of the night playing flute and tenor sax.

It made me feel good, as a long-time Basie fan, to see the Count perform before a full house of young people. Fairfield is a small town in the cornbelt but everyone there seemed to dig Basie's jazz.

Jan. 28 1964:

The band opened with a bouncer, "Easy Money," in its first one-nighter in Gulfport,Ill. "Moon River" gave the sax section of Marshall Royal, Eric Dixon, Charlie Folkes, Foster and Wess a chance to strut. "All of Me," ignited by a salvo from Sonny Payne's drums, got everyone's attention.

Basie followed with Royal's lush solo on "What Kind of Fool Am I?" "One O'Clock Jump" ended the first set.

Back on stage, the band delivered two of its jukebox hits, "April In Paris," with its catchy ending, and a thunderous "I Can't Stop Loving You."

Leon Thomas came the stand to unleash the blues on "Every Day," a number made famous by Joe Williams. He also shouted "Disillusioned Blues" and a rip-snorting "Git!" Oddly, the blues made the audience happy.

Dancers hit the floor as the tempo was relaxed for "Nice and Easy," "I Left My Heart In San Francisco," "Teach Me Tonight" and a cool "Mint Julep."

Someone asked for Dixieland. I cringed a bit, doubting if Basie would do it. He obliged, though, as several of the brassmen joined in on, I think, "Jazz Me Blues." Maybe it was "Royal Garden Blues" or something else. Anyway, it was done quickly and very well.

Basie's band was headed into a string of one-nighters around Chicago, then to Ohio, prior to a Kennedy Foundation concert at New York's Americana Hotel that was postponed after JFK's assassination.

After New York, Basie reported, the band would tour Florida and then do a benefit in Southern California with Mahalia Jackson, Dean Martin, Frank Sinatra and Sammy Davis, Jr.

The Count had just one problem of consequence in January, 1964. "I'm looking for someone to take over the first horn in my trumpet section," he said. The trumpets sounded extremely good to me that night, but I wasn't there to find fault. I was a reporter more than a critic. An awful lot would have had to be wrong for me to recognize it, especially amid all the supper club commotion.

Aug. 25, 1964:

Basie, traveling with the caliber of band that had kept him at the top of the heap for three decades, got things rolling with "Jumpin' at the Woodside," sparked by tenor honkings and brayings of Sal Nistico, who had been on the same bandstand with Woody Herman late in 1963.

"I Can't Stop Loving You," given impact from Payne's pounding and the band's potent brass, with four trumpets and as many trombones, made the 250 fans of the Count's music forget that the dance began two hours late.

Thomas, a young man with an easy-going style, was wearing a lace-trimmed shirt that was, someone insisted, "too much" for the cornbelt crowd. He had added some moxie since January, it seemed. His features included Ellington's "I'm Just a Lucky So and So."

Royal was featured on a ballad that was, Basie announced, scored by Billy Byers. Back in the rafter-shaking mode, the band roared through "Take the A Train," embellished by Dixon's flute, and an encore of "April In Paris."

Basie turned romantic after the smoke had cleared. The interlude included "Indian Summer" and "Sophisticated Lady," to the approval of the dancers. The beat went on as the band glided through two of the Count's hits, "Moon River" and "I Left My Heart In San Francisco."

After a break, the crew came back with "Swinging the Blues," a Basie fixture since the thirties, and the more recent "Shiny Stockings." Dixon then teamed up with Wess for a light-hearted run through "The Swinging Shepherd Blues."

"Sleep," played as a shouter, gave Nistico, who had replaced Foster in the reed Section, a workout that allowed him four at-length solo breaks. His honkings earned him some applause and whistles. It was a drinking crowd that was, nevertheless, well-versed about Basie's music.

There was more where that came from. The band followed up with "Ol Man River," featuring the unwavering tubster, Payne. This number almost matched the thunder and lightning going on outdoors during the evening. Drum solos are crowd pleasers, I know. But they can get monotonous and pointless if allowed to drone on too long. Payne's major value, I thought, was his solid, relentless beat, not his solos. I loved his crackling rim-shots.

Basie gave us a treat by featuring himself on several long solos, picking up the rhythm section as he moved along. He did more with a few well-placed "plinks" and "plunks" than many pianists can with a fusillade of ornate runs.

He was like a watercolorist, I've thought, who uses white space to advantage instead of filling all his paper with paint. His suspenseful pauses were, I figured, Basie's white space.

Because the band's plane from Kansas City had been delayed, the performance didn't end until 3 a.m., instead of the usual 1 a.m. finish. So, naturally, there was some kidding about the birth of a new Basie closer: "Three O'Clock Jump."

Basie's last appearance in Burlington was at the Pzazz! night club in 1972. He played dance tunes for the most part, with only a few fast numbers. Al Grey was outstanding with trombone solos on just about every tune.

My last opportunity to see Basie was on Sunday, Sept. 6 1981, when he appeared for "Basie Night" at the Chicago Jazz Festival.

The Count, who had to use a powered cart to go on and off the stage, was cheered by an estimated 80,000 people.

In addition to the Basie band, the reunion featured Williams shouting the blues on "Every Day" and some other favorites of his. He was backed by inspired solos from Eddie ("Lockjaw") Davis, Warren, Tate, Edison and Newman.

Warren, obviously elated, led the Basie grads through "Broadway" and "Swinging the Blues." Solo honors went to Edison, I thought, for his exquisite "Georgia On My Mind."

Larry Kart, writing for The Chicago Tribune, pointed out that the alumni had "proved that the rhythmic lessons Basie taught cannot be unlearned."

Apr. 26, 1984:

I had put a stack of Basie LPs on turntable that morning, instead of Goodman, Oscar Peterson or Zoot Sims.

While driving to work there was bad news on my car radio: "Count Basie is dead at age 79 . . . "

My mind went back to when I was a teen-ager, putting nickels in jukeboxes for "Basie Boogie" or "Cherokee."

I remembered the smoky Paradise Club and, of course, the time I saved the Count's life with a pack of Chesterfields.

Once, I recalled, I asked Basie if it bothered him to see "pirated" records by his band in the stores, with no royalties for him. "Not really," he said. "There's no way I can fight it. And it means that many more people get to hear our music."

# Stan Kenton

My first chance to see Stan Kenton's band was in early October, 1944, at the RKO Theater near Boston's infamous Scollay Square, a risque area young GIs such as myself had been warned to avoid.

I was more interested in hot music than wild women anyway. So I went to the RKO, along with a guy from Oklahoma who leaned more toward Roy Acuff. It was an exciting show with the hipster, Anita O'Day, doing such tunes as "Are You Livin' Old Man?" and some kind of rambling "blues." Karl George provided some impressive straight-on trumpet breaks.

Our outfit was headed to Europe on the Aquitania in a few days. Being able to see Kenton, instead of an "ickie" band that could have been at the theater, was a real kick.

Quite a bit transpired, including the Battle of the Bulge and V-J Day, before I got to see Kenton again. This was on Nov. 10, 1948, in the Burlington Auditorium.

There was a huge, boisterous crowd for the Kenton crew that night with the "Artistry In Rhythm" gang doing SRO business across the country.

Iowa was fertile territory for Kenton. Stan's personnel included, I believe, such standouts as Buddy Childers, Ray Wetzel, Chico Alverez and Conte Candoli in the trumpet section and Harry Forbes, Harry Betts, Harry DiVito and Bart Varsalona playing trombones. Art Pepper, George Weidler, Bob Cooper, Warner Weidler and Bob Gioga were in the sax section, as well as I can recall. The rhythm section included guitarist Laurindo Almeida, bassist Eddie Safranski, drummer Shelly Manne and, on bongos, Jack Costanzo.

June Christy, looking radiant in a low-cut white gown and purring with a voice as sexy as Lizabeth Scott's, was what jazz fans used to refer to as "an absolute gas."

Kenton came back to Burlington in 1966. I was entertainment chairman for Steamboat Days and insisted on some contemporary jazz, not just Dixieland. Stan had reorganized after a layoff and had a band without "names." We paid $3,500, which wasn't too steep for a Saturday night.

It was a good feeling to pay Kenton, with quite a wad of cash, and talk with him in his dressing room. He was doing one-nighters, traveling by bus, and seemed to be bushed. He was very nice to deal with. He didn't bat an eye, in fact, when I asked him to do two 90-minute shows, a format not spelled out in our contract. We were only charging "a badge and a buck" and this gave us a chance to bring the eager Kenton fans through the gate twice.

"Limehouse Blues," in a brassy arrangement by Bill Holman that was loud enough to clear anyone's sinuses, opened both concerts. The rest of the fare was, for the most part, lush ballads such as "All the Things You Are," "You Stepped Out of a Dream" and "But Beautiful." There was some jazz, such as "Peanut Vendor" and "Intermission Riff." But it was mostly ballads, though there was no dance. It was a precise band, as I remember it after nearly 30 years. I was all over the place that night as a reporter, photographer and paymaster. There was no time for detailed notes.

Kenton bands appeared at the Pzazz! night club twice in the early seventies. Stan couldn't make it to one of the dances, due to an apparent health problem. But the band was on its good behavior and played beautifully. The top soloists, I thought, were baritone saxophonist Chuck Carter on "Rhapsody In Blue" and altoist Quin Davis, eloquent on "What Are You Doing the Rest of Your Life?"

Trumpeter Mike Vax, trombonist Dick Sherer, saxophonist Willie Maiden and drummer John Von Ohlen also drew raves from overflow crowds in the club's Tiger Pit, a venue reminiscent of South Tahoe or Las Vegas.

Some jazz fans didn't come to see Kenton. They had heard some of his complex, "wild" numbers and figured he was too progressive. Kenton played many styles of music over the years, from Wagner to "West Side Story" to the rock tunes identified with "Chicago." All of it wasn't a howling success and some of it was hardly jazz. But his outfit was as good as anyone's when in a swinging groove and deserved an open-minded hearing.

Kenton, who was 65 by the time, brought his 19-piece band to Hancher Auditorium on Jan. 25, 1978, and played to a packed house of 2,884 at Iowa City.

"The audience at the two-hour concert was made up of both young and old," T. J. Ryder noted in a review for The Des Moines Register, "and though it was enthusiastic, it was not ecstatic."

Packed houses were "infrequent" at Hancher, on the University of Iowa campus, and a spokesman said the turnout was proof of "the powerful drawing ability of Kenton, recognized as a leading force in jazz for 40 years."

I did take notes at Iowa City and they told me the evening began with "Body and Soul" and ended with "Intermission Riff," an interpretation I hadn't heard before. Kirk Smith, a new bassist, played it with what I recall as having a country swing movement in it. It was kind of a shock to hear him, after Eddie Safranski and his successors, but it worked. I looked forward to the band cutting some records with the new sound that was, it turned out, provided by a bassist who seems to have disappeared from the jazz scene.

The band played all its standard fare with the booming tenor sax of Roy Reynolds propelling "Yesterdays," the bongo drums of Ramon Lopez driving "Bogota" and the screeching trumpet of Steve Campos punctuating "Peanut Vendor," Michael Bard's penetrating alto was excellent, in the tradition of Kenton's many fine altoists, on "Street of Dreams." Cooper was back with his husky baritone solo on "Rhapsody In Blue."

Kenton had suffered a skull fracture in a fall at Reading, Penna., on May 22, 1977, and his lagging health led to some off-and-on itineraries for the band. He obviously was not in good health at Iowa City. I realized this when I talked to him backstage after the concert. He autographed a self-published book of mine that included a photo my wife took of me with Stan on Cape Cod in 1975. Creative World had bought a copy of "Encore" in 1977.

The Register devoted a sidebar story to the troubles endured by Stan. It noted that he had entered the concert hall alone, after his sidemen dashed in from the bus, and that he "walked slowly and stiffly."

"I never get tired of one-nighters," Kenton told writer Jerald Heth. "But I just haven't been able to get my strength back since the (brain) surgery." Nevertheless, he said he would continue to travel during the summer with, he expected, a tour of Great Britain in October, 1978.

Kenton's health problems had mounted by the time he came to Mt. Pleasant, Ia., for a concert at Iowa Wesleyan College. It was a rainy Saturday night, Apr. 22, 1978. Stan still looked good, with his big frame and handsome features, but he had trouble speaking clearly when announcing what the band was going to play. I asked him to do their new, symphonic arrangement of Billy Strayhorn's "Chelsea Bridge," which had been performed at Iowa City. "Oh yes, he replied, seeming a bit disoriented. "Chelsea . . ."

They played "Chelsea Bridge," a fine chart by Alan Yankee that was never recorded, in flawless fashion. The band did well all night, though there were only a few hundred people in Cottrell Gym. When I talked to trombonist Roger Homefield and other band members during the intermission I could detect a feeling that all wasn't well in the realm of Kentonia. Maybe it was just the fact the band was in a small Iowa town on a Saturday night, not in Los Angeles. Some of the musicians seemed uncertain about the future.

I managed to get a so-so tape of the performance on my recorder. It was a slightly different band than at Iowa City.

Kirk Smith had been replaced by John Ward on bass and two young women, whose names I didn't catch, had succeeded Pete Asch and Yankee in the sax section.

Reynolds was impressive with his strong flute solo on "Peanut Vendor" and I got a kick out of the sax section's unity on Hank Levy's "A Time for Love."

Kenton died on Aug. 25, 1979. I reacted with a column in The Des Moines County News, reprinted in Dr. William F. Lee's "Artistry In Rhythm" book:

The St. Louis Cardinals had just won a squeaker from the Dodgers on the West Coast and I tuned my radio for the 1 a.m. newscast. I forgot the ballgame when a terse ABC bulletin reported that "bandleader Stan Kenton has died in a Hollywood hospital . . ."

Stan's death was a shock but not a real surprise, I noted. He had been ailing two year and had, I pointed out, faltered at least twice in attempts to take his exciting "Artistry In Rhythm" orchestra on the road to resume the kind of one-nighters he did for 40 years.

But it was difficult to accept Stan's death, even though my acquaintance with him wasn't intimate. I put a stack of his LPs on my phonograph Sunday morning and recalled some of the things that made me so thankful he had lived.

Over the years, Stan maintained his prestige as a leader, arranger and composer. He always reflected his integrity while touring the world, including some small Iowa communities, to play concerts and dance dates. Somehow, he found time to do clinics for teen-age musical hopefuls.

There was a note of pride for me when the Kenton band played for Steamboat Days, and also some humor. I recall hovering behind Stan to take his picture while he was playing the piano. "I always think you guys are trying to catch me when I'm picking my nose," he quipped. During the intermission, I asked him why he wasn't using a bongo drummer. "It would cost too much," he said. "We'd have to pull the equipment in a trailer behind the bus. It all gets back to money. Everything in life gets back to money, you know."

Before getting married in 1973, I found out that Millie shared my fondness for "good" music. We were able to see Kenton eight times in Iowa, Illinois and Massachusetts.

Someone's birthday was being celebrated the Sunday night we saw the band in a Chinese restaurant in West Yarmouth. I think it was Audree Coke, the public relations manager at Creative World.

The band was never up tight. But it was in an especially mellow, relaxed mood as we listened to it from the bar. When we opted to stay for the second show the bartender rang the tab up as if we had ordered another round of drinks. "This," I thought out loud, "is the way to live."

We had hoped to see the band in England in the fall of 1978, while noting our fifth wedding anniversary. But the tour was cancelled due to Stan's health complications.

After hearing the newscast I remembered the Sunday afternoon at Geneseo, Ill., when Stan had to play what he referred to as a "toy" piano in the high school gym. He kept his composure, even though the pink upright wouldn't let him hit some of the notes he reached for on such numbers as "Send In the Clowns."

I remembered the night we drove home from Iowa City, blazing a trail through a falling snow, after Stan's concert. The music was great but it was sad to realize he was a sick man.

Also, I remembered Art Hodes telling me about the night in Springfield, Mo., when he and Kenton were booked into the same complex for a college prom. "There was only one piano," Art said, "and he let me use it."

Stan deplored the self pity generated by hillbilly music, as played by untutored guitar twangers. But he did all he could to help serious musicians advance their careers.

He was a gifted man. But I will always recall him as a hard, uncompromising worker. It required a lot of toil and financial risk for him to attain worldwide fame.

It was right, I think, for Kenton's will to stipulate that there be no "ghost bands" traveling around as "the Stan Kenton orchestra." His music was unique in jazz. No one should be able to claim it after his death, if that's the way he wanted it. (End of newspaper column that was published on Sept. 6, 1979).

"Ghost bands" are one thing and tributes are another. The Bieds went to Newport Beach, Calif., in the fall of 1991 when the 50th anniversary of the Kenton band was celebrated "where it all began," at Balboa Beach.

Actually, the concerts were held at the nearby Hyatt Newporter. But the Kenton fans attending the "Back To Balboa" event, including 18 concerts, toured the area where the Rendezvous Ballroom stood. We also attended a one-nighter by Shorty Rogers' big band in a restaurant overlooking the bay.

About 40 former Kenton performers were at the reunion: Maynard Ferguson, Bud Shank, Bill Perkins, Jack Costanzo, Bob Cooper, Chris Connor, Anita O'Day, Bob Gioga, Buddy Childers and others. Vic Lewis came from England and he conducted a band of Long Beach students in a medley of some of Kenton's progressive charts. Tom Talbert, who had done some arrangements for Stan, was on the bill with a subtle, swinging crew that offered contrast from the louder bands. Tom's rendition of Ellington's "Bojangles" was outstanding.

O'Day sang "And Her Tears Flowed Like Wine," reminiscent of 1944. Lee Konitz did his exquisite "Lover Man" on alto sax. The alumni band played "Eager Beaver," naturally, with gusto added via six trumpets and six trombones. The volume was reduced by several decibels for "Interlude," featuring guitarist Almeida as composer Pete Rugolo conducted. The sound was immense.

There were panel discussions, with pathos and humor, which focused on Kenton's devotion to music and revealed why so many of his sidemen considered him "a father figure."

One of the musicians, a trombonist, told about the time Stan disclosed the need for a pay cut so he could afford to do a series of clinics for students. "I had a job lined up for more money playing in a Broadway show," he remembered. "But after thinking about it overnight I decided to stay with the band."

Life was tough with Kenton on the one-nighter trail. "We traveled until we felt like we were numb," another alumnus said. "But it was worth all of it when the curtain went up each night wherever we were. It was worth it just to hear the sound of our theme . . ."

# Harry James

It was a big night in the small town of West Point. Ia, when Harry James and his band came in for a dance at the Legion Club. The date was Apr. 9, 1959.

Duke Ellington's one-nighter at West Point in 1953 was no dull event. Fats Waller had played in the town in the thirties. But one of the dance hall's habitues gave James a verbal bouquet , if that's what it was, when he said the Music Makers had drawn "the biggest crowd we've had since Tiny Hill."

James had "dropped a blockbuster" on the Legion Club with his impressive 16-piece band, I reported in a column published in The Hawk Eye the following Sunday. "It was just about the best, and maybe the loudest, music heard in these parts since Duke Ellington played in Burlington in 1948," I wrote. "One thing is certain; James hasn't lost any of his enthusiasm or his technique. The guy still swings!"

This was remarkable, I thought, considering that he had been on the one-nighter trails much of the time since joining Ben Pollack in 1935. Also, I opined, the celebrated trumpeter could had probably quit music for a life of retirement at his new Las Vegas home "if so inclined."

This was, in retrospect, a foolish observation in view of James' obvious passion for jazz. He needed income, too, in order to finance a lifestyle that included playing the horses.

In addition to James, the band, billed as "the new James," was sparked by drummer Jackie Mills, alto saxman Willie Smith and a library of Basie-oriented charts from the talented Ernie Wilkins.

Some of the old favorites, such as "Who's Sorry Now?" and "Cherry," were still featured. But the bulk of the band's repertoire that night was a departure from what HJ played in the thirties and forties.

One incident stands out in my mind from that night some 35 years ago: a guy who resembled "Mister Five by Five" blew up a storm jitterbugging with a svelte woman directly in front of the bandstand. James, who was in the midst of a fiery solo on a jump tune, got to laughing so hard he had to quit blowing and watch.

I offered my praise, as a jazz buff with a weekend forum, to James and to the Legion Club for what proved to be a top-drawer show in an unlikely venue for jazz.

The only slip-up worthy of mention was an inadequate sound system which made it tough to hear vocalist Jilla Webb over the band's high-decibel brass section.

Mills was no wallflower, either. His drums had a big role in drowning out Webb's vocalisms. It was a loud band in a small arena, of course. The celebrants around the club, myself included, made a lot of unsyncopated racket.

My column quoted Walker Cox, a good friend who had been a staunch James enthusiast since around 1938, as saying his idol hadn't aged in the past decade. "Being married to Betty Grable must agree with Harry," my pal mused.

What I wrote ended with an announcement that the Les Brown band would be at West Point in a month. There was also a quip from a jazz addict, Hubert Flockman, who hoped the Legion would book Artie Shaw and his "all wife orchestra" for a dance.

James had played his first dance date in Burlington around 1949, with a fine band propelled by drummer Don Lamond after his duty with Woody Herman. That one-nighter drew a huge crowd, probably 1,500 or more, to the auditorium. HJ played at Pzazz! in 1972, also drawing a wall-to-wall turnout.

I had seen the Music Makers at the Aragon in Chicago around 1943 and was at the WGN studio when the band did a Chesterfield broadcast with Helen Forrest and Johnny

McAfee doing vocals. After the war, when James played at the Trianon on the South Side, the place was so jammed it was almost unbelievable. I didn't dream the big band era would hit bottom in a few years.

James was a "survivor." His band was at Cedar Rapids and also at Davenport around 1960. Harry was very obliging at Davenport when asked to pose for a photo with Cox. He was in a rush to get to the band's bus but still polite enough to smile for "just one more."

Cancer was fatal to James on July 5, 1983, at Las Vegas, where he'd lived since 1959. Four of his children were present when he died, including two from his 20-year marriage to Grable, a pin-up favorite during World War II.

The Associated Press referred to James as "one of the last great talents of the big band era" and noted that the band was continuing to play in California.

"To me," James had said in a 1980 interview, "there are no old times, only today. I don't like to talk about what we used to do. I like to talk about what we're going to do."

Solos he played with the Goodman band around 1937-38 still sound exciting to me. I have purchased the recordings in the 78, LP, cassette and CD formats. What'll be next?

# Woody Herman

Woody Herman came to our town in 1940 with his originial band, the one that "played the blues."

He played Southeast Iowa throughout the forties, an area sometimes dismissed as being "the sticks," and was still very popular around Burlington, Iowa City and other towns with ballrooms, or dance halls, well into the eighties.

In 1966, when I was involved with Steamboat Days, the Herman band was booked for a concert and dance. We announced him too soon and had to change our ads when Woody, through his agent, cancelled the date. So we booked Stan Kenton and Buddy Defranco's Glenn Miller band. "Touche!"

In 1967, we tossed caution to the wind and booked the Herman band again, the contract specifying a concert plus a dance. I figured he could feature a few soloists for the concert and then follow it with dance music. We advertised it that way and agreed to pay $3,500 for the Saturday night appearance.

I mentioned the concert to Woody. But he refused to do it, explaining that he knew "what they want to hear." He had a good band with Cecil Payne on baritone sax, Carl Pruitt on bass and Sal Nistico on tenor sax.

Woody's bus driver, a savvy kind of guy, told us we were foolish to charge only "a badge and a buck" for admittance that night. "They'd pay $10 to see this band," he said. He was right, but we were locked into the $1 figure across the board and couldn't change it for the Herman dance.

The band warmed up some old chestnuts, such as "Greasy Sack Blues," and pleased all of us with Woody's warm vocal on "Laura." He played too much clarinet, perhaps, but his saxwork was good enough to even the score.

Herman packed the auditorium, despite the fact that the big band era was "dead."

One reason we wanted Herman was because he had been a hit on Nov. 18 1963, in a one-nighter at Gulfport, Ill. My review of that gig appeared in The Hawk Eye the day President Kennedy was slain. I'm not sure if anyone read it or not.

"Herman, now 50, buzzed into town around 6:30 p.m. in a black Chevy sport car," I reported. "His arrival was followed by a bus load of his musicians, most of them appearing to be just beyond their teens."

Herman's car was a new Corvette. His previous one, with a plastic body, had been wrecked. He told me it was the first time he ever had an accident in which the car went "squish."

Skipping his "Blue Flame" theme, Herman got the night underway with a cool version of "Wine and Roses" in what, I think, used to be referred to as "a businessman's bounce."

It was a very good arrangement, popular on the radio and on some jukeboxes around Southeast Iowa. "It was only exceeded," I wrote, "by another playing of it later in the night after the band had warmed up."

The interim was filled with such numbers as "Rose Room," featuring Woody's alto sax, and the reed section's velvety number, "Midnight Sun." The band's five trumpet players, prodded by heat from Nick Brignola's baritone horn, filled the dance floor with a medley that included Duke Ellington's "Don't Get Around Much Anymore."

To prove they could do anything if they set their minds to it, the bandsmen played a free-for-all rendition of "The Twist." It featured a tall, lanky high-note trumpter, Bill Chase.

"Sister Sadie," a speeding vehicle for tenorman Nistico, who resembled Vido Musso but sounded like Paul

Gonsalves,found him shouting for attention the way Gonsalves did at Newport on "Crescendo In Blue."

Ellington's "Satin Doll" featured the saxes and some energetic strumming by bassist Chuck Andrus. This was followed by a 1963 version of "Jazz Me Blues." The warhorse never had a better outing.

The orchestra played "Woodchopper's Ball," of course. Another high point of the evening, during which dozens of people had to be turned away at the door, was "Watermelon Man." The Latin-flavored tune featured Nistico's husky tenor, Chase's strident trumpet and Henry Southall's to-the-point trombone.

Nat Pierce, the band's pianist and arranger, seemed to enjoy his added role of nudging the band's youngsters as they played what were, in some cases, new and difficult charts.

Phil Wilson's urgent trombone was in the spotlight on "Mood Indigo." He was, I noted, "a master with the kind of plunger that emits an eerie 'do-wah' tone."

Chase was just as impressive, I thought, on his "I Can't Get Started" tribute to Bunny Berigan. The brass section took command en masse on "Ol' Man River" and a blaring "One O'Clock Jump."

Herman, a fine balladeer, sang "Pennies From Heaven," "I've Got the World On a String" and, as usual, "Laura." The band's vintage year, 1945, was recalled by "Apple Honey," played as fast and forcefully as ever, and the bombastic "Caldonia." (Does anyone but me remember that Erskine Hawkins cut the first record of this tune?)

During an intermission, Herman lauded the club's efforts to keep big bands alive. "There's no reason the Midwest shouldn't have live attractions," said Herman, a native of Milwaukee. "The tube is getting pretty tiresome. People want to see the entertainers in person."

One of Herman's fans, a business woman from Burlington who enjoyed greeting celebrities, asked Woody how long he had been in the band business. "About 105 years," he quipped.

Undeterred, she asked if he had writted any music. "None you'd want to listed to," he fired back.

Herman offered a surprising comment. "It's easier to be a jazz fan than a musician," he said. "It's more fun to listen to music than it is to play it."

NOTE: I was among the Woody Herman fans attending the "Early Autumn" reprise of his career in September, 1993, at Newport Beach, Calif. It was a grand event with fine music from the bands of Bill Holman, Shorty Rogers, Terry Gibbs, Bill Perkins and Frank Tiberi, leading a present-day Herman band that impressed everyone with its spirit and expertise.

Woody was talked about in great detail during panel discussions in which his ex-sidemen and others recalled a man they obviously admired. He could be awfully tight with money, they agreed, and he sometimes drank too much and was known to fire a musician on the stand. He kept going over the years, though, and was obviously the kind of guy most jazzmen appreciated as a boss and, importantly, as "one of us."

One of Herman's former road managers said Woody pretty much ignored his mounting tax problems in the early eighties. "That's how he kept the band going," he explained.

# Louis Armstrong

Item one, my review in The Burlington Hawk Eye began: the mid-July mormon fly attacks along Burlington's riverfront can be devastating.

Item two: the auditorium's new air conditioning unit is working A-OK.

Item three: everyone who enjoys good humor and spirited jazz loves Louis Armstrong.

The Burlington Steamboat Days jazz show on July 17, 1964, with a crowd estimated at 3,200 people in bleachers and camp chairs on the riverfront, got swinging around 9:25 p.m. when Art Hodes and his combo dashed off a peppy rendition of "Royal Garden Blues."

Applause and foot-tapping were heavy. A light attack of mormon flies was underway.

Hodes and his crew, including trumpter Whitey Myrick, clarinetist Jimmy Granato, trombonist Danny Williams, bassist Earl Murphy and drummer Red Saunders, paraded through "St. James Infirmary Blues." Williams' ribald trombone smears and witty vocal paced "I Wish I Could Shimmy Like My Sister Kate."

The applause was nearly drowned out by the flapping wings of the pesky insects, also known as May flies, as they marshaled their forces for a full-scale invasion.

Hodes finished his set with "Washington and Lee Swing," then evacuated the premises in favor of the New Wine Singers.

The group performed well, dishing out a mixture of folk songs and one-liners. One ditty in particular, "The Adolf Eichmann Stomp," rang some bells.

By 10 p.m., though, the bugs had become a maelstrom and the emcee, Nip Nelson, advised the crowd: "Let's get the hell outa here!" The bugs slickened the turf, but most of the 3,200 made it to the auditorium in nothing flat.

The New Wine Singers and Nelson picked up where they'd left off on the indoor stage. People sat on the floor or in balcony seats, glad to be able to applaud rather than swat at the flies.

Then, to the strains of "Sleepy Time Down South," the Armstrong combo took charge, I noted, "like Al Capone's mobsters intimidating an old guy with a pushcart." From here on it was Satchmo's show.

Arvel Shaw's bowed bass, Eddie Shulman's mellow clarinet, Russell ("Big Chief") Moore's gutsy trombone and Armstrong's trumpet, making up in warmth what it might have lost in overpowering technique, led the way through a rousing "Back Home Again In Indiana."

King Louis sang "I've Got a Lot of Livin' To Do." after a huge ovation the group, with Billy Kyle at the keyboard and Danny Barcelona on drums, whizzed through "Tiger Rag."

Armstrong, in typical good humor, sang a song that had to do with the birth of jazz in New Orleans. Kyle, an impeccable pianist with a strong bass hand, was spotlighted on "When I Grow Too Old To Dream," which is seldom heard in jazz concerts, and Duke Ellington's familiar "Perdido."

Then, to no one's surprise, Armstrong sang his current hit, "Hello Dolly," using the second or third of the eight handkerchiefs used during the night. Someone backstage actually counted the handkerchiefs. "They're not just a gimmick." Hodes told me after the show. "He really sweats that much during a concert."

Shulman, a graduate of the Goodman school of playing jazz clarinet, offered a round tone and a steady drive in his feature, "On the Alamo." Shaw, a big man who played with the tenderness of a kitten at times, was highlighted on "Royal Garden Blues." Then Armstrong brought the house down again singing "Blueberry Hill."

Moore, who measured about five-by-five, got his turn to shine on "Ja Da," opening with a dramatic flourish that was like an overture. He iced the cake playing the melody in nimble fashion and doing a vocal in an amusing, whispered style.

Shaw was featured again on "How High the Moon," Armstrong sang "Mack the Knife" and Barcelona slashed and flailed his way through a fast-paced "Stompin' at the Savoy."

Jewel Brown, stunning in a sparkling blouse over a skin-tight skirt that might have been sprayed on, then stopped traffic with an uptempo "Lover Come Back To Me." She encored with "Can't Help Lovin' That Man," reminiscent of Billie Holiday, and a romping "Billy Bailey."

It was 12:45 a.m. by this time. Armstrong and his group were looking forward to a 300-mile overnight bus ride to Storm Lake, Ia. So the show ended as the Armstrong combo, joined by Hodes and his band, got together on a thundering "When the Saints Go Marching In."

I'd tried to interview Armstrong during the intermission but a protective road manager said King Louis was too tired to be quizzed. He did, however, play some at a nearby night club before the bus left town.

Armstrong was at the top of his popularity in the summer of 1964, thanks to "Hello Dolly." He was paid a fee of $4,500 for his night's work. The figure was nearly a third of the entertainment budget for the entire event.

# Artie Shaw

I didn't get to see Artie Shaw in his hey-day.

So I never got to hear him play the clarinet in person. Some jazz fans thought he was better than Benny Goodman.

I was never ready to concede that, but figured it was a double-treat to have both of them on the scene. Choosing between Artie and Benny was, to my notion, about like being forced to decide between Lana Turner and Linda Darnell. Why quibble?

Shaw went back on the road for a while, minus his licorice stick. The band appeared for two concerts at the Medinah Temple in Chicago on Apr. 28, 1984.

My wife and I were there for the Saturday afternoon performance by the 16-piece orchestra with Dick Johnson playing the clarinet as Artie watched, very intently, from just off the bandstand.

Shaw was known as being aloof, if not downright antisocial, in the forties; especially when the jitterbugs and other "ickies" got in his hair. Once, in 1939, he had left in a huff to hibernate in Mexico. But he was back in a few months to record "Frenesi," which enjoyed 19 weeks at the top of the charts.

Only about 200 people were on hand for the matinee, and another slim crowd that night. It seemed to embarrass the guy from a radio station who introduced Shaw. Artie performed like a champ, though. He had a ball narrating what the band was up to during the show. The program included 19 tunes, plus three bonus playings of "Nightmare," the band's theme.

Shaw joked some. But he was very serious about the music performed under his name. He didn't allude to the 1,500 or so empty seats. (During a similar situation at the Burlington Auditorium in the forties, Victor Borge told the audience he would have invited them to his hotel room if he had known so few of them would have been on hand).

Shaw went into detail about some of the numbers that had been fixtures in his book. "Rose Room," he said, was the arrangement that epitomized the way he wanted his band to sound in the late thirties.

It was obvious that Shaw was proud of the band. He extended lavish praise to Johnson who, it turned out, was able to approach Artie's high-note solos on such tunes as "Traffic Jam."

The Gramercy Five was revived in 1984 with Joe Cohn, the son of jazz great Al Cohn, on guitar. The band-within-a-band played "Cross Your Heart" and "Summit Ridge Drive," hits from around 1940, in grand style. The small group was expanded as the Trafalgar Seven to do a modern "Milestones" and a classical "Jazz Suite for Clarinet," giving Johnson a chance to show that he had been uptown.

"Traffic Jam" and "Back Bay Shuffle" were both presented in extended form, continuing after their original three-minute formats. The old arrangements, the correct length for 78-rpm records, were used on "S'Wonderful," "Dancing In the Dark," "Moonray," "Stardust," "Moonglow," "Temptation," "I Surrender Dear," "Begin the Beguine," "Any Old Time" and "What Is This Thing Called Love?"

The music sounded great to me and it drew bursts of applause from the satisfied customers. Shaw seemed very happy, maintaining his enthusiasm during the two-hour span. Members of the band, most of them too young to recall Shaw as a player, went all-out to give a professional performance.

John McDonough, the Chicago-based jazz writer and critic, made it clear during the intermission, and again on the way out, that he was impressed by what we heard.

One thing bothered me a little. Some numbers such as "Frenesi," which was distinctive because of violin, cello and viola instrumentation, didn't sound quite right with only saxes and brass.

Nothing was bad about it. But I've heard those tunes hundreds of times over the years with strings and Shaw, more than anyone, knew how to use strings in the swing era context. "Frenesi" still sounds fresh to me after all this time, even without strings. This is certainly a tribute to the arranger, William Grant Still.

The best tune of the concert was, I think, "Rose Room," which had an infectious beat and exactly the right tempo. It was introduced as the band's prototype; what's good enough for Artie Shaw is good enough for me.

# Lionel Hampton

Lionel Hampton brought his big band, plus a vocalist and tap dancer Bunny Briggs, to the Hotel Burlington on Sunday, June 19, 1977. It was a favor to a local friend, Elmyra Benhart, and the St. John AME church. The church was in need of funds and Hampton played for what Elmyra described as "a very, very reasonable fee."

Hampton is quite a guy. In addition to being the best ever to play the vibes, in my opinion, he headed some outstanding record dates in the thirties. He joined with Benny Goodman to help erase the color line in jazz and has kept a big band on the road much of the time since 1941.

Lionel is a wealthy man, according to reports, ranking high in GOP political circles, an unusual dimension for a jazz performer. But when I met him in '77 he was as humble as anyone I could imagine. When I asked him to pose for a photo with a friend, Walker Cox, he acted as though he was supposed to do it.

The big band went through its paces for an hour before Hampton appeared in the ballroom. What had been a yawner of a concert suddenly caught fire as the jazz legend entered the room.

He blazed away at the vibes, and at the drums, for a couple of hours. The invigorated band blew mightily on such barnburners as "Air Mail Special" and, of course, "Flying Home."

I got to spend some time with Hampton in the fall of 1990 when he appeared on the SS Norway. The week-long voyage was dedicated to Lionel as producer Hank O'Neal noted that "his 60-year career in the spotlight on center stage continues and his energy and musicality remain undiminished."

Away from the spotlight, Hampton could have easily disappeared in the crowd. He did blend into the ship's routine, at times, when I saw him at a slot machine (near one of my wife patronized at some length) in a corner of the casino. He looked very good, sporting the "rug" Dorothy Donegan enjoys kidding about. Millie asked him to pose for a photo with me on St. Thomas and he anxiously complied.

I respect Hampton too much to have gotten pushy with him when we talked. We kept it at the "small talk" level and, after some years of wondering, I asked him who the "Till Tom" was in the 1940 record by the Goodman Sextet, "Till Tom Special." I thought he might have been an evangelist. "No," Lionel corrected, "he was more of a practitioner around Los Angeles in the thirties." He was, apparently, a "healer" of the type was had in Iowa during the Depression years.

Hampton showed his age, which was 81 at the time, when he had trouble climbing the steps to the stage in the ship's Saga Theater. On stage, he shuffled as much as he walked. He told some jokes, rather awkwardly, and blew a couple of punchlines as if he had done it before.

Suddenly, when the spotlight hit him, he stroked the vibes with all the poise and beauty he had displayed in 1936 at the Steel Pier or on Jan. 16, 1938, at Carnegie Hall.

There was, of course, a huge ovation from the crowd. Terry Gibbs and Gary Burton played some fine vibes, also. But it was Hamp's show. When he did "Flying Home," and such other specialties as "If the Blues Was Whiskey" and the mandatory "Hey Baba Rebop," the honored guest was backed by a 20-piece band.

The sidemen, rehearsed especially for the occasion, included trumpeter Jon Faddis, trombonists Al and Mike Grey, pianist Kenny Barron, bassist Keter Betts, drummer Bobby Durham and congo drummer Gabriel Machado. Milt Hinton, who had lingered in the wings, came on stage as "special guest bassist." The big crowd hooted, stomped its feet and howled.

I don't enjoy brassy music as much as I did before 50 years of being in the infantry, working around printing presses and listening to torrents of jazz. My favorite selection by Lionel that afternoon was his soft, swinging solo on "Over the Rainbow." It was, I thought, the best music during the cruise.

Hampton played two programs on the Norway. Each of them featured different numbers so people seeing both shows, as I did, got a double-barreled treat. He did "Midnight Sun" in one show and "Misty" in the other.

"The crowd went bananas," I reported in a post-cruise article. "He played the drums, sat in a while at the piano, to Barron's delight, and sang a couple of numbers to make sure the audience didn't get short-changed," I wrote.

There has been no shortage of tributes to Hampton in recent years. Applause and good reviews are probably his best tonics. I was glad to see Lionel booked into the Ravinia Festival near Chicago in 1991 and was impressed by the raves he got from Howard Reich in The Chicago Tribune.

"He still plays vibes with energy and finesse," Reich reported. "His improvisations on Gershwin's 'Our Love Is Here To Stay' were melodically beguiling, his version of 'April In Paris' harmonically cunning." Reich was correct, I believe, in crediting Hampton's orchestra as being"the longest-running band in jazz history."

Hamp is also revered overseas. The entertainment lounge on the main floor of the Meridien Hotel in Paris is, my wife and I noted in 1988, now known as the Lionel Hampton Jazz Club.

# Al Hall

There always seemed to be something special about the way Al Hall played bass, usually with a smile on his face and always with a relentless beat.

Al, who was born in 1915, was with Benny Goodman's band on the "Camel Caravan" show in 1939 and was a CBS staffer on radio shows featuring Mildred Bailey, Frank Sinatra and the Tommy Dorsey band. He was on TV with NBC's "Today Show," working with such legends as violinist Joe Venuti, and played on Broadway in such hits as "Music Man," "Fidler On the Roof" and "High Button Shoes."

Al recorded with Duke Ellington, Teddy Wilson, Mary Lou Williams, Erroll Garner, Eddie Condon, Billie Holiday, Sarah Vaughn, Libby Holman and Pearl Bailey, to name a few, and was with both Ellington and Goodman at the Rainbow Grill.

I met Al at Sweet Basil in 1984. He looked familiar to me when he came in carrying his bass, bobbing and weaving through the crowd to the bandstand. "Aren't you Al Hall," I asked, "who played with Benny Goodman on the 'Camel Caravan?' " Al was able to talk, after removing his overcoat, and told me it was nice to still be recognized after a long career that had, I think, hit at least one of its peaks in 1977 during a concert tour in France, Switzerland and Germany.

Millie and I were going to New York a lot in the eighties and always looked forward to seeing and hearing Al at Sweet Basil with Doc Cheatham's group. We developed a "pen pal" sort of relationship. He invited us to his West Side apartment and when he died of cancer on Jan. 18, 1988, we received a telegram from Wilma Dobie, one of Al's best friends, telling us the bad news.

Alfred W. Hall was born in Jacksonville, Fla., and grew up in Philadelphia. He began playing cello at age eight, then took up the double bass with hopes of a career in symphonic music. That wasn't to be, however, because symphonies weren't hiring blacks in that era.

Al "scuffled," performing around New York with, among many others, Ellis Larkins, Kenny Clarke, Count Basie, Phil Moore, Eubie Blake, Dexter Gordon, Ben Webster and Tiny Grimes. He had accompanied Alberta Hunter as a young man and when she resumed her career as a blues singer, in 1978, he joined her at the Cookery.

Al taught music, in addition to playing it, and once owned a business known as Wax Records. In 1946, when he joined the orchestra for "Barefoot Boy With Cheek," he was the first black musician in a Broadway pit orchestra, according to one of his daughters.

"The cash register is ringing favorably (at Sweet Basil) so I guess the management is satisfied," Al informed me in a letter he wrote on Aug. 9, 1986, to keep me posted on what we had been missing around the Village. "Doc Cheatham has been out of commission for eight weeks with a double hernia operation. We've had Spanky Davis, Earle Warren and Irving Stokes during his absence. Monday, I go to Aspen with the dance group called 'The Copesetics,' from the old Cotton Club days. A week's engagement and back to Sweet Basil. Love to your wife and give me an advance notice of your next visit and have dinner with us."

Al enclosed some things he had written for a newsletter published by Dobie's Overseas Club. He wrote well, in impish fashion. One of his items, "Popcorn Fantasy," was accompanied by a sketch by his wife, Elizabeth, an accomplished artist and teacher. "Recently I felt that I had exhausted my supply of fantasies," Al wrote. "Just now, one has been pecking at the gray matter. I feel like the mother hen just about to lay the ultimate Easter Egg! Or, maybe that legendary goose that laid the golden egg."

It came to mind, he explained, while he was watching Elizabeth popping corn. "What if those kernels were all musical notes and could be contained? What a fantastic musical score they might pop up with. Take B-flat, for instance. It would have different meaning to different performers. To Pavarotti it would sound and mean one thing; Billie Holiday would give it a soulful meaning; then Frank Sinatra would take it in his special way; Ben Webster would make it blue . . . what if I could just take that B-flat and split it. Well, it could probably take us into the fifth dimension. And, man, maybe that's what the Fifth Dimension is all about!"

Al also wrote some jazz history. In "Mirror, Mirror On the Wall," he told about playing cello, violin and tuba until his ears "perked up" to the sounds of Louis Armstrong in 1932.

"I have transcended every phase of this business called music," Al wrote. "House bassist with Decca Records when they were known as 'Race Records' and very much in vogue with Cow Cow Davenport, Johnny Temple, Josh White and his 'One Meat Ball,' Louis Jordan, Sammy Price, Joe Turner, etc. My own Wax Records label featured Ben Webster, Denzil Best, Jimmy Jones, Dick Vance and Al Casey in 1946."

Al went on to recall playing with such international stars as Jean Sablon, Josephine Baker and Django Reinhardt at Cafe Society Uptown. All of this, he mentioned, had begun when he was the novice in an eight-piece band at a Pennsylvania roadhouse where Al could learn his craft but not speak his mind. "Shut up," they would tell him. "You're still wet behind the ears!"

Rev. John Garcia Gensel, known as the pastor to the jazz community, visited Al several times while he was hospitalized. "No praying," Dobie wrote to me. "He does that within himself." Dobie pointed out that Al was "a very proud man and I know he doesn't like being clucked over."

Al's memorial service was held Jan. 23, 1988, at St. Peter's church on Lexington Avenue, with the Rev. Gensel presiding. There was music by Cheatham, Chuck Folds, Jackie Williams, Ted Sturgis, Laurel Watson, Linda Fennimore and

Brooks Kerr. Robert C. Maynard, the Oakland publisher who was Al's son-in-law, delivered remarks.

We didn't make it to the service, being 1,000 miles away. We sent a "cheery note" to Al, at Dobie's request, a few weeks before he died.

"I gave him the column about jazz you'd sent to me," she wrote. "He enjoyed it, I'm sure."

# Red Norvo

I had seen Red Norvo perform with Benny Goodman in 1945, and at Rick's Cafe in Chicago during 1977, but didn't meet him until October, 1990, on the Norway.

Lionel Hampton, Terry Gibbs and Gary Burton were on the same cruise, guaranteeing that the ship's "vibraphone spectacular" would be just that. But Norvo, who always insisted on calling his instrument a vibraharp, got an ovation when he played a brief "When You're Smiling" with just one hand.

Norvo, at age 82, was on the cruise as a guest and not as a working musician. He had suffered a stroke, apparently, and needed some help getting around. His mind was sharp, though. He was extremely friendly and anxious to talk about some of his musical memories.

I mentioned Red's hometown, Beardstown, Ill., which is 100 or so miles south of Burlington. He was born on Mar. 31, 1908, and his real name was Kenneth Norville. I read that in a jazz directory many years ago and also read that his father played piano and sang. With the piano, Red reported, he played "mostly chords."

Norvo grinned when I reminded him of the "destruction of the vibes" stunt I saw him do with Goodman at the Chicago Theater. This was just after V-E Day. Red was featured with the Sextet, which was pictured the next week in Life magazine with Red at the vibes. The full band cut loose with "Gotta Be This or That," with a slapstick role for Norvo.

The comedy routine, which was the ultimate show-stopper, seemed to be inspired by an act Norvo and BG might have seen in a vaudeville show. Red got angry as he played, swinging at the vibes with mock ferocity as Goodman yelled "Get it Red, get it!" He finally whaled away at the vibes with mallets nearly as large as boxing gloves before ripping the apparatus apart, strewing the keys on the floor.

Then, with the situation well out of hand, Goodman fetched a fire extinguisher from backstage as Red went for an axe. All of us in the seats went bananas.

Norvo, whose underrated band once featured the arrangements of Eddie Sauter, told me he thought some of Benny's most impressive solos were written out for him by Sauter. He meant "Clarinet A La King," I assumed. He also mentioned "Clarinade," a feature while Norvo was with the 1945 band.

Norvo's career has been documented in several books: his remarkable 1933 recording of "In a Mist" with Red playing marimba and BG on the bass clarinet, his marriage to Mildred Bailey when they were known as "Mr. and Mrs. Swing," his key role in Woody Herman's band in the mid-forties and his modernist period with such be-bop innovators as Charlie Parker and Dizzy Gillespie.

Red was in a more conventional mode in the fall of 1977, however, when playing at Rick's Cafe. The club had many inspired bookings in the seventies, arranged by pianist Bill Snyder who performed in a revolving dining room atop the Holiday Inn.

Norvo appeared with pianist Dave McKenna, cornetist Warren Vaché and tenorman Scott Hamilton. They featured some of the swing era anthems Red had helped popularize in the thirties and forties.

I remember Norvo doing one the Bix's tunes, either "Candlelights" or "In the Dark," with some improvisational touches. He seemed happy doing such tunes as "Rockin' Chair" and "Tea For Two" pretty much the way he played them when he was on the way up. From the heart.

Norvo was always a soft player, except when he was "destructing" his vibes, with abundant dexterity, skill and feeling. He relied on thoughful ideas, not just sheer volume and energy, to express his years-ahead styling of standard tunes.

He came from an era of jazz individualists and was, luckily for jazz fans, always his "own man."

# Lee Castle

Lee Castle came about as close as anyone, I thought, in filling the void left by Bunny Berigan's death in June, 1942.

That was my opinion as, a year or so later, I was into jazz far enough to pick some favorites. I was impressed by Castle's hard-driving trumpet on "Basin Street Boogie," a sizzling Columbia platter by Will Bradley's Six Texas Hotdogs.

By 1943, Castle was in the brass section of a fine Goodman band that featured such other veteran jazzmen as Jess Stacy, Hymie Schertzer, Gene Krupa and Miff Mole. The brash, uncluttered solos Castle took with this band reminded me of Berigan when, on nights there was no static in the air, I heard Benny's broadcasts from the Hotel New Yorker and/ or Astor Roof.

Castle also played with Tommy Dorsey, Artie Shaw, Glenn Miller, Red Norvo, and Jack Teagarden. He came to Burlington twice, leading his own bands, for a supper club one-nighter in 1963 and a Steamboat Days dance in 1984.

The band kicked off with "Just You, Just Me" the night it played at Grandinetti's. It followed up with such familiar numbers as "Gypsy In My Soul" and "Perfidia."

Castle surprised me when he sang, in able enough fashion, as the band played "Just In Time" and "Brother Bill." His blonde vocalist, Marilyn Mitchell, pleased me even more. Her style was compelling and she was fun to watch as she delivered some of the era's pop tunes.

Castle's appearance at the club launched a big band policy that led to engagements by Duke Ellington, Count Basie, Woody Herman and other top-notch ensembles. The place held about 250 customers, if all of them sat down at once. People came and went that night and my review in The Hawk Eye reported an overblown figure of 350 attendees. It was a permissible lie, I reasoned, since Castle's band was very professional and a good report on him would help drum up even beter things. Hyperbole is part of "show biz."

"This isn't the Palladium," one of Castle's sidemen had quipped when he stepped out of the band's bus in the parking lot. "But we've played in smaller places." The club was a roadhouse, pure and simple. It had clean restrooms, a place to change clothes and a bandstand larger than some I have seen in famous clubs in Chicago and New York.

"Big bands are making a comeback," Castle, who was 48 at the time, told me. I reminded him of when he played with BG in 1943. He reminded me that his brother, Charlie Castaldo, was a trombonist in the same band. Castle was born as Aniello Castaldo and he became Lee Castle on the advice of a booking agent.

Castle was 70 years old and recovering from heart surgery when he returned to Burlington in 1984. The band was doing Jimmy Dorsey tunes, for the most part, but also playing such standards as "Sweet Georgia Brown" and "Deep Purple." The arrangements were typical of the forties.

He was still playing well, especially on ballads. I told a friend I thought he was "still as good as most anyone" but pointed out that Castle never gained national fame because there is only space for a few performers "at the top."

One of the dancers asked Castle to play a Glenn Miller tune, "anything by Glenn Miller." Firmly, he replied: "Miller didn't play Dorsey tunes and we don't play Miller tunes." Castle was with Miller a while in 1939, then joined Tommy Dorsey and roomed with Frank Sinatra on the road.

"It's a grind," Castle said when I asked him about the band business. He only had a few days of notice about the Burlington job after an abrupt cancellation by Woody Herman. "We have to hang loose," he remarked.

I complimented Castle on the band. It was well-rehearsed and enthusiastic even though the date was on what had appeared to be an off night, a break in "the grind."

"Thanks," he responded. "I wouldn't go out on the road with anything I didn't consider to be a good band. But there are times I think it might be best if I'd throw it all in and quit."

Castle's band and a later performance by Buddy Morrow's Tommy Dorsey band in Burlington prompted me to write an editorial defending "ghost bands" with, of course, some reservations.

"They have to be staffed by musicians competent enough to do justice to the original leaders," I pointed out. Going on the road with an inferior band would be an injustice to Miller or the Dorseys.

"It's a bit like the St. Louis Cardinals," I wrote. "Stan Musial has been retired since 1963 but the Cardinals have been in the World Series four times since he quit."

# The Bob Cats

Yank Lawson, Eddie Miller and Ray Bauduc were among my musical heroes in the early forties, ranking right up there with Count Basie among the performers I enjoyed.

So it was a treat on Mar. 23, 1985, when I found myself in an elevator with Lawson, Miller and Bauduc at the Sheraton Hotel in St. Louis. They were in the city for a reunion of Bob Crosby's Bob Cats that highlighted the fourth annual Mid-America Jazz Festival, ably produced by Charlie Wells.

"The acts ran from terrific to mediocre," a reviewer for The St. Louis Post Dispatch opined.

"Fortunately, far more were terrific." He made it clear the revival of the Bob Cats, a formidable jazz force from the mid-thirties to around 1942, was a notable success.

The authentic Bob Cats in St. Louis included Lawson, age 74 at the time, on trumpet and Bob Haggart, age 71, on bass. Bauduc, the drummer, was 78, and tenorman Miller was 74. Nappy Lamare, who played guitar and sang, was 78, and he was also present for the get-together. The former Crosby stalwarts were joined by clarinetist Johnny Mince , pianist Ralph Sutton and trombonist George Masso. It was, truly, an "all star" band.

Masso led the way on opening night with "The Basin Street Blues." Haggart joined Bauduc, solid as ever with his crackling rim-shots, on a romping "Carolina In the Morning."

Miller's beautiful, distinctive tone was still evident as he calmed things down with his timeless rendering of a forties ballad, "Dream," that was penned by Johnny Mercer.

I had seen Miller in the hotel's coffee shop earlier in the day and asked him, in kidding fashion, if he was still up to playing a barnburner, "Call Me a Taxi." He had recorded the tune in 1938 with Haggart, Bauduc and two-fisted pianist Bob Zurke. Miller's comeback was: "Sheesh!"

Haggart and Bauduc brought down the house with "Big Noise From Winnetka," always a joy to see and hear although they could have phoned it in from their rooms. The band ended its first set with a blaring "South Rampart Street Parade," never a favorite of mine but a meal ticket for Dixieland performers as long as I can recall.

It was remarkable, I thought, how fresh the familiar tunes played by the Bob Cats were in the hands of the enthused old pros. For me, this kind of music needs to be heard "live" to get the feel of it. I enjoyed it even more, especially the Dixieland, when I used to drink. All the "boom, boom, boom" gave me a lift.

Bauduc, Miller and Lamare were all "gone" within a few years after their 1985 reunion. They were natives of New Orleans, a good place to learn jazz. Bauduc left for Chicago in 1924, Miller went to New York in 1930. Lamare, nicknamed by Miller because his blues solos on guitar tended to put Eddie "to sleep," migrated to New York in 1928. George T. Simon once lauded Miller as "one of the greatest tenor saxists of all time." No one could top the beauty of his tone.

Haggart, in great shape when I saw him in recent years, was honored in Florida on his 80th birthday in March, 1994. Lawson had shown more age, certainly. He was still blowing his horn in convincing, if not overwhelming, fashion when I heard him at Sarasota in 1992.

I talked to Wells while assembling "Jazz Memories." He said the reunion of the Bob Cats was "the high point" of his career as a jazz producer. "We had hoped to bring Jess Stacy in from California," he said, "but he didn't feel up to flying."

Sutton was, of course, an excellent choice as pianist with the Bob Cats. He was paired with Jay McShann that weekend as "the last of the whorehouse piano players." My recollections include a solo on "I Found a New Baby" by Sutton that was a masterpiece in impeccable delivery.

I never got to see Bob Crosby's band in person, though the Blackhawk in downtown Chicago was one of its frequent bases of operation. This was before I was a jazz fan, so I had to settle for second-hand reports about such legends as Zurke and clarinetist Irving Fazola, who impressed one friend of mine with his capacity for gin.

"Faz" was a tremendous player with an unrivaled tone I admired on such Crosby platters as "Sympathy" and, with Claude Thornhill, a too brief but gorgeous solo on "Autumn Nocturne."

It is a very good thing when producers such as Charlie Wells are willing to do the hard work, and take the financial risk, to stage such inspired jazz shows as the one that reunited the Bob Cats.

When I talked to him in 1994, Charlie was excited about an upcoming tribute to Benny Goodman with Peanuts Hucko, Peter Appleyard and Frankie Capp. Right on!

I had given up on ever seeing the Bob Cats and agreed with the St. Louis reviewer, Dick Richmond, that they were "terrific." In retrospect, his disappointment with the New Black Eagle trad band could have had something to do with all the excitement over the Bob Cats, who "stole the show."

One lingering memory: riding in an elevator car with three aging Bob Cats was about as intimate as any jazz recollection could get.

# Ray McKinley

The four trumpets sounded like "four panes of glass breaking at once," I noted in my review of Ray McKinley's Glenn Miller band on Dec. 12, 1963.

"The audience listened," I reported. "It danced, listened, danced and danced. there were some tears. They all applauded and cheered."

My report on the one-nighter in Gulfport, Ill., continued by reminding that the original Miller Army Air Force band, with McKinley on drums, had a "big" sound that was enhanced by a violin section. Otherwise, the unit McKinley was fronting two decades after the war was comparable to the one in the ETO.

McKinley's 18-piece crew opened with "Moonlight Serenade," as Miller might have in the forties. After a few bars of the familiar theme, the band played a sparkling rendition of "Satin Doll." It was, I realized, more than just a "ghost band."

"The Song Is You" was followed by "My Prayer." McKinley left the drums to sing "My Kind of Girl" in his warm, rhythmic style. Next, there was a medley that included "Perfidia," "September Song," "I Left My Heart In San Francisco" and, for the Miller buffs, "Sun Valley Jump."

Joan Shepherd, a nifty-looking vocalist, came on for "Moon River" and "Almost Like Being In Love." Someone near the bandstand pointed out, perhaps with accuracy, that "she probably hadn't been born when Glenn Miller died."

"Old Black Magic," "Misty," Tuxedo Junction," "Frenesi," "String of Pearls" and "Don't Be that Way," all given a lift by the band's potent brass section, delighted the crowd.

The dancing stopped when McKinley delivered a drum solo that, I thought, was well-constructed and not too long. It had substance, not just noise.

McKinley and his entourage had rolled into town around 7 p.m. in a yellow bus. Tiny Hill, the town marshal, had provided an escort from the Mississippi River bridge, complete with a low siren moan as the bus pulled up to the club, which was owned by Tiny's daughter and her husband.

"I'll have your best steak," McKinley told the waitress in his Texas drawl. "Medium rare."

He checked the bandstand, terming it "the smallest I'll play on all night," and reported that the band business was "picking up." His band, at any rate, was getting "plenty of bookings."

McKinley had tried to shed the Miller image, he told me. "But the people won't let us." As a compromise, the band mixed a few Miller tunes with a format of swing era numbers.

"You won't hear much new," said the man who, in the late forties, fronted a progressive orchestra that featured the stylish arrangements of Eddie Sauter.

McKinley praised such sidemen as trumpeters Lou Lantz and Eddie Zandy, clarinet and saxman Steve Cole and tenorman Bruce DeMoll. While his vocalist poured herself into a wine-colored gown, he talked about his World War II broadcasts to GIs. "We got bombed out of London," he reminded me. "We just played there one night a week, then moved around to different bases."

In 1963, McKinley was looking for a "modern formula" for his band. "If we play 39 tunes by Glenn Miller and leave one of them out we're bound to make somebody sore," he lamented.

McKinley and his band had a date the next night in Austin, Minn., about 300 miles north of Burlington. The one-nighter was his third local appearance in four years with a large, enthusiastic crowd each time.

# Si Zentner

"If you think it's loud out there," bandleader Si Zentner yelled to no one in particular, "you ought to try it up here. It's so noisy I can't stand it!"

Zentner, an excellent trombonist with a Las Vegas flair for humor, was in Gulfport, Ill., for a one-nighter on Dec. 3, 1963.

He drew about 200 people. Not bad, really, for a small town on a Monday night when most of the supper club's regulars were resting up from their weekend rigors in the area's temples of mirth. Few of them had heard of Si, except for seeing some ads and a few mentions in my newspaper columns.

Zentner's band seemed to be in an upward mode. They swung from the heels that night for what he referred to as "a small group of dedicated music lovers." The opening tune, a bouncing "Like Young," sported a Lunceford-like beat that set the night's agenda. "Ebb Tide" was much the same, reminiscent of a Basie or Sam Donahue arrangement.

The band's pre-yule bag of musical gifts included such favorites as "Heart and Soul" and Sy Oliver's "Yes, Indeed!" The trombone choir reminded me of Trummy Young and his sidekicks on Lunceford's rendition of "Mandy."

A brass-laden flagwaver, "Little Jazz," was dedicated to trumpet great Roy Eldridge. The "sex" section, as Zentner called it, was featured on a mellow "Stella By Starlight" that captured the Kenton mood. It was followed by an ambitious production number, "Liberation," that chased the dancers from the floor. The selection was a 15-minute dose of modern jazz that was an unusual treat in the Dixieland belt.

Along with its musical savvy, the Zentner band impressed me with its enthusiasm. As one saxman took a solo, for instance, a couple of others would jump up, horns at ready, as if to "cut" him.

Zentner's humor was infectious. When he played an especially good solo his three section players feigned disgust and began to take their sliphorns apart.

Zentner, who had something to say between each number, proved to be the funniest bandleader I have seen.

"Most bands play a medley of tunes by the swing era bands around this time of night," he noted shortly before midnight. "That's kind of dumb, isn't it? We'll play a medley of our number one hit." The band kicked off "Up a Lazy River," its claim to fame on the jukeboxes in other parts of the country.

"Count Basie says we have the greatest white band going," Zentner declared around 1 a.m.

The Count, who was due at the club in a month, would have his hands full topping Zentner's performance for the "small group of dedicated music lovers," I wrote the following Sunday.

Woody Herman was coming in a week, I reminded, "and he'll have his work cut out for him in this regard."

Zentner's band returned for a Steamboat Days dance in 1966, when I was entertainment chairman. Only a few hundred people showed up. But the band did a fine job, as I knew it would, still playing in the tradition of Lunceford, Basie, and Donahue much of the time. The sidemen, all unknown to me, were superb.

Zentner was, I guess, in the right place at the wrong time. His band would have been a sensation during World War II, about the time most of the sidemen were born.

# GI Jive

Thirty-four hundred tapping feet added up to 1,700 delighted "good old days" music fans at the previous night's concert by the US Army's Jazz Ambassadors, I reported in the Burlington Hawk Eye on Oct. 5, 1990.

The 18-piece band, in Burlington under the newspaper's auspices, touched most of the revered musical bases from John Philip Sousa to Duke Ellington, I noted, along with the contemporary sounds of Matt Catingub.

The Jazz Ambassadors, led by Chief Warrant Officer Charles L. Booker, Jr., had played in all 50 states and at jazzfests in Europe, I added, including the major Nice, Montreaux and North Sea events.

"Focus," a bouncer Count Basie would have loved, kicked the concert off on the right foot. Penned by sax section leader Gene Thorne, the number featured a booting tenor sax solo by Pat Dillon, accented by blaring riffs from the band's five trumpets and four trombones. Greg Reese added a bold chorus on fluegelhorn. The band was already in the groove.

Slowing down to ballad tempo, the Ambassadors showcased Tom Williams in "Invitation," a fluegelhorn tour de force. The soloist, who had played with the bands of Mercer Ellington and Ray Charles prior to his Army career, pleased Booker, the band and the entire crowd.

Next, there was a big band tribute including hits by the Goodman, Miller, Kenton, Ellington, James and Dorsey bands. Kenton, Ellington, James and TD had made the original sounds on the Burlington Auditorium's stage, I pointed out in my review.

"Trilogy," a progressive chart by the band's Vince Norman, featured the ensemble's lilting woodwinds, potent brass and a lively soprano sax solo by Loran McClung. The band, all sergeants and many of them with a decade of service, joined in a rousing climax after impressive solos by Williams and trombonist Jim Falls.

Delores King Williams, an attractive woman with a voice to match, just about stopped the show with her animated rendition of "Hey, Look Me Over." Williams, as good as many of today's well-known vocalists, continued with a medley of such World War II hits as "White Cliffs of Dover" and "Boogie Woogie Bugle Boy." She was joined by Richard Aspel, who also toiled in the brass section, in a tear-jerking "We'll Meet Again." My eyes got moist, at any rate.

After a 20-minute break to smoke or whatever, the band returned with a shouting performance of Catingub's "Blues and the Abscessed Tooth." Fred Hughes, who pounded out a piano solo, shared the spotlight with tenorman Norman and the band's tasteful (no long solos all night) drummer, Tom Dupin.

Ellington's "Mood Indigo," in a clever arrangement by Thorne that flirted with an uptempo beat, featured trombonist Lewis Chapman. His plunger mute gave the tune a Cotton Club flair.

It wouldn't have been a jazz concert in Burlington without Dixieland. So the whole band saluted the era of Bix with a peppy "When the Saints Go Marching In." The number recalled the spirit of Burlington Steamboat Days, launched in 1963 as a Dixieland festival but taken over in recent years by rock and country sounds.

It wasn't jazz, perhaps. But vocalist Williams, whose hubby was the band's gifted fluegelhorn soloist, returned for a sentimental "The Wind Beneath My Wings' which, she noted, was from a movie called "Beaches." Aspel and bassist Willie Barber then made it a vocal trio doing a funky, funny "Opposites Attract."

The concert ended, except for two encores, with a swinging version of Sousa's "Stars and Stripes Forever" that reminded me of when, around 1946, the Goodman band played "Under the Double Eagle."

Much better than swinging the classics, in my opinion. (BG called it "Benjie's Bubble.") "In the Mood," the first encore, featured a tenor sax battle done pretty much the way Tex Beneke and Al Klink did it with Glenn Miller. Peanuts Hucko and Jack Ferrier waged it in the ETO.

"God Bless America," delivered with gusto by Williams, was embellished by a flurry of notes from baritone saxophonist Daryl Brenzel. The crowd responded with a "standing O," then marched to the parking lot.

# *a medley of Jazz Photos*

*Peggy Lee and Benny Goodman on stage in 1942.*

*BG blowing someone else's horn in the forties.*

*Benny Goodman with the author on July 2, 1948.*

*Wardell Gray in Iowa with the Goodman bop band.*

*Cootie Williams and Duke Ellington in '71 concert.*

*Harry James and drummer Don Lamond at 1949 dance.*

*Billy Kyle plays 'Perdido' during concert in 1964.*

*Woody Herman plays 'Rose Room' on Nov. 18, 1963.*

*Doc Cheatham, Barrett Deems, Art Hodes, Bud Freeman.*

*Hillard Brown and Art Hodes during mall concert.*

*Peter Nero during Civic Music rehearsal in 1965.*

*Earl Hines, jazz piano great, in circa 1975 pose.*

*Anita O'Day at Jazz Showcase on May 5, 1990.*

*Stan Kenton at Steamboat Days in summer of 1966.*

*Eddie Miller and Ray Bauduc at St. Louis in 1985.*

*Billy Butterfield plays "What's New?" at Condon's.*

*Eddie Condon's jazz club awaits wrecking ball.*

*Red Allen at the Metropole in September of 1963.*

*Wild Bill Davison at Pizza Express.*

*Rene Franc plays at the Slow Club in Paris.*

*Peanuts Hucko, Mel Powell, Ray McKinley in 1988.*

*Red Norvo on the Norway in October of 1990.*

*Doc Cheatham and Wynton Marsalis in 1988.*

*John Bunch at Eddie Condon's in June of 1988.*

*Louis Armstrong and Leonard Brooks in 1964.*

*Al and Elizabeth Hall pose at Sweet Basil.*

# *Pianists and some Singers*

# Leonard Brooks

The first time I heard Leonard Brooks play piano was in a place called the Palace Inn, located two blocks from the Mississippi River in Burlington, Ia. It was in 1942. I was a teenager and the tavern, which had a Wurlitzer upright on a small stage near the front window, was "off limits" to me, in the eyes of the law.

My sister, Bette, was a fan of swing era music who used to listen to Fletcher Henderson and Earl Hines from Chicago when she was in high school. She took me to see Leonard, a gent with the reputation of being "a swinger." The bartender overlooked the fact that, legally speaking, I belonged in an ice cream parlor, not a gin mill.

Bette gave Leonard the sheet music to "In a Mist," by Bix Beiderbecke. After a few tries, he played parts of it reasonable well and with some evidence of what was to be known as "soul." Bix was from Davenport, just upriver from Burlington, and his reputation was known around town as his mystique grew during the thirties and forties.

Leonard was a showman, on top of being an exciting pianist. Something like Fats Waller or Earl Hines. He actually resembled Hines in appearance, also in his style at the keyboard.

His rollicking version of "Blues In the Night," a hit at that time, was preceded by an introduction that sounded like what I had heard the calliope players do from atop the Streckfus steamboats. From that night on I have felt that jazz should be happy music, for the most part, not a dirge. Sad, mournful music belongs in a funeral home or a church, I think.

As years went by, including World War II and my fulltime writing career, I kept remembering the night I heard Leonard Brooks play at "the P-I."

I remembered the way his notes seemed to explode and then fly around the room when Leonard played "Tea For Two" or "Honeysuckle Rose." He played some schmaltz, too, when a drunk demanded it. But Leonard was a jazzman. He followed the melody, as a rule, and enhanced it with tasteful, ornate runs. He had vigor, with remarkable skill for a man without a whole lot of formal training.

I didn't see Leonard or hear anything about him until an afternoon in 1964, when our paper had been "put to bed." I was in a bar at Gulfport, Ill., when a guy wearing what appeared to be a raccoon coat dropped in to use the phone. I knew it was Leonard, almost immediately, and introduced myself. "You used to be Leonard Brooks," I joked. "I came in to hear you play 'Blues In the Night' at the Palace Inn."

Leonard was between jobs. So I phoned Betty Grandinetti, whose club featured some jazz. "I know a piano player you'd love," I gushed.

Leonard auditioned the next night, wearing a tux, and was impressive. He loved the spotlight. "I am the star," he would remind his fans, "I am the star," he would repeat. Then he would prove it with chorus after chorus of inspired melodies. He often capped a set of uptempo numbers with "a little Rodgers & Hart."

There was a lot of drinking where Leonard played. He could handle the stuff but took some kidding about it as his fans kept sending drinks to him, including some he didn't consume. Leonard wore thick glasses and one night a patron asked if he was blind. "He usually is around 2 in the morning," the bartender cracked.

I found out that Leonard, or "Lenny," was raised in Fort Madison, known as "the pen city" because it is the home of the Sheaffer Pen Co. It is also the site of the state penitentiary, if that matters. Leonard learned about music in local schools, someone told me, and also in the church his family attended.

After a year at Gulfport, Leonard moved his one-man show to downtown Burlington. He signed on at the Arion club, owned by a friend of mine, Art Diewold. The Arion was a family cafe, not a jazz club. But a lot of the Arion's customers enjoyed jazz.

Leonard knew how to entertain salesmen, including some who "cried in their beer" when hearing Irish tunes. He played "Melancholy Baby," of course, and "You Made Me Love You." One of his specialities, "Alley Cat," was a nightly must if playing a tune three times qualified as a must. He had to yell the lyrics, at times, to be heard over the noise at the bar.

Amid all the hokum there was a feel of jazz. Bunny Berigan put jazz into every note he blew. Leonard did pretty much the same thing at the piano. He was a natural.

My favorite song was "The Days of Wine and Roses," around 1965. Leonard played it wistfully, as it was written, but with a sly bounce the way George Shearing or Jess Stacy might do it, if so inclined. He actually had two ways of playing it, for lovers and for jazz buffs. Liberace or Roger Williams couldn't have done "Roses" as well, in my opinion, in the "pretty" vein.

The last time I saw Leonard was at the Arion bar. It was late on a weekday afternoon, around 1968, and he was moving to Southern California to play and also do some composing and/or arranging. He had taught young people for a while in Burlington and wanted to do some music with a religious theme and, I think, some youth involvement.

It choked me some to hear Leonard play "Wine and Roses" for the last time, reminding me of a friend who had died. I thanked him, of course, and thanked him for the concert he played without charge during a one-man art show I'd held in 1965 at the Hotel Burlington.

We talked about a lot of things, including the night I asked him to come to the auditorium and play during intermission when Woody Herman performed at Steamboat Days. His selections included "a little Rodgers & Hart."

I gave Leonard one of my watercolors. He played a bit more of my last request, "Roses," in a tempo that just about forced me to tap my toe without knowing I was doing it. We shook hands, said "so long" and that was it.

We exchanged a couple of notes while Leonard lived at Santa Barbara. He phoned me in February, 1980, just to talk and to tell me he was ill.

I phoned later in the month to see how he was doing. His son, also "Lenny," answered. Leonard and I had an emotional exchange. He told me he had gone deeply into religious music, with a jazz perspective, in a church in Santa Barbara.

I talked to Leonard, Jr., a while. "I'm also a piano player," he said. He was, I think, still a pre-teen.

When I wrote something for print about Leonard's death on Feb. 21, 1980, I speculated about him joining Bix, Earl Hines and Louis Armstrong, who knew Leonard, for "a jam session in the sky."

That was far-fetched, I suppose. But I know Gabriel would like Leonard's music if they ever do meet.

# Art Hodes

Art Hodes died, at age 88, on Mar. 4, 1993, after a long illness.

The next day I was interviewed at a local radio station, KCPS, to talk about a friendship with Art that went back to July 25-27, 1963, when he helped launch Burlington Steamboat Days.

"I bought some of his records around 1942 when I was in high school," I began. "He was in Burlington a dozen times over the years, including the four times he played for me. He had a strong left hand and a critic with the New Yorker magazine said he was probably the most intense blues player of all time."

Art's style wasn't comparable with Art Tatum or Oscar Peterson in technique, I admitted. "But he influenced a lot of jazz pianists, such as Dick Wellstood. I can hear something of Art in the style of Marcus Roberts and I have some records by Thelonious Monk doing ballads in a style like Art's. I asked Art about this once and he said Monk used to drop in when he was playing at clubs in New York."

Hodes had an audition to play for Benny Goodman's band. "But he really didn't have his heart in it," I said. "He thought it would have been like playing fifth typewriter in an ensemble of Remingtons and Smith Coronas."

I told the interviewer that Hodes "did it all" in jazz. "He was a piano player, a composer, a bandleader, a disc jockey, a teacher, a lecturer and the author of many articles as well as two very good books."

On top of that, I said: "He was a good neighbor to the people he knew and an outstanding family man. He lived pretty much like other people except he had a piano in his house and he traveled all over the word playing jazz."

Back to 1963:

Art had the original "house" band for the event, serving as the anchor for a lineup that included the Dukes of Dixieland, then headed by the Asunto family, and the band of Doc Evans. The band Art brought from Chicago included trumpeter Whitey Myrick, trombonist Dave Raspberry, clarinetist Jimmy Granato and drummer Red Saunders, who had gained some fame playing at the Club De Lisa. In Chicago, the band played regularly on Rush Street at, I believe, a place called Bourbon Street.

Hodes turned out to be the most popular "name" entertainer in Burlington history with more SBD appearances in 1964, 1965, 1969, 1974, 1976, 1981 and 1987 when I hosted a retirement party and unveiled "My Kind of Town."

We kept in touch over the years with letters, brief notes and a few phone calls. Art was anxious to play in Burlington, where he was always well received. He got weary of long trips to Europe, Australia and Canada as time went on and his health problems piled up.

"Just back from Europe," he wrote on June 10, 1976. "England, Belgium and then Germany. It was rush, rush, rush. Go to your hotel and grab a fast bite. Off to the theater to perform. Find a place to eat. To bed, then up. Back on the bus. It was all hurry, hurry . . .

"But I want to relate about Berlin, where we played in the best hall I can remember playing in. Berlin Philharmonic Hall, where their symphony performs. I couldn't begin to describe the hall except to say that there were 4,500 people in the place and I didn't feel crowded in any way.

"I stood at a window and looked out where I knew the Berlin Wall was, maybe less than a mile from where I was performing, and it was hard to contain the welled up feelings in me.

"Here I was, free to be, and there they were doing it the hard way. And when I traveled through the East German zone, in order to play our next town, I was sure of it. Yes, we should all have the opportunity of traveling through a bit of communist country to appreciate what we in America have."

Everywhere he played, Art added, "the response was the same. Standing applause and much kindness shown to us. Europe certainly has a love and appreciation of our American jazz and its masters. But Dan, as you know, there's no place like the good old USA. See you soon."

In 1977, the University of California Press published Art's impressive book, "Selections From the Gutter," a collection of first-hand reminisces by and about such jazz figures as Cow Cow Davenport, Bunk Johnson, Omer Simeon, Pops Foster, Gene Sedric and Hodes himself.

"So I sat in with Bix," Art recalled in one of the articles, 'and we jammed 'til early morn when Bose relieved him. I remember Bob Conselman was on drums. When we'd stop to rest Bix would fool around a little at the piano. No one made a sound 'til we finished playing. Then the house resounded with applause."

Art's band lasted 11 weeks at the Blue Note in Chicago, he related in another article. "I can't recall all the name groups that played opposite us. I do remember Sarah Vaughan being there. Probably Erroll Garner. This was the top jazz club in Chicago (in January, 1950). The agent had a great plan but looking back it didn't have much chance to succeeded (booking a Dixieland band along with big name jazz). I couldn't stand too much of that excitement. O'Brien, Brunis, Collins, Pee Wee, all gone now. But they made big music while they were here."

The book, including some good photos, is still the best of its type I've seen. "That was the time of the two fisted piano player," Art wrote in remembering Chicago's fabled South Side. "You had to make it on your own. No drums and bass to support you. It was all your own gig . . . no mikes, no amps. Yeh! We had a day, and we had an age. Well the giants have been here and gone. We have recordings, and we have our stories to tell."

I hired Art in early October, 1980, to promote my new "Backstage Burlington" book with shopping mall and downtown appearances. He brought Hillard Brown, who had played drums briefly with Duke Ellington, and Jeep Robinson, a tenor saxophonist with good rhythm and a fat tone, for the gig. They drove from Chicago, nearly a 500-mile trip both ways with Art driving his van and Hillard's drums and cymbals crammed behind them.

"In the Mood" was the opener at the mall, where a lot of shoppers came an went as they played. Some stood and listened, though, as the combo did spirited renditions of "Chicago," "Basin Street Blues," "I Can't Get Started," "Back Home Again In Indiana" and Jelly Roll Morton's "Grandpa's Spells," my pick from among all of Art's specialties. I always got a kick out of him banging his elbows on the keyboard on that number.

I'd hoped for friendly weather in October but it was windy and cold the next day when the group played from a gazebo near a bank with some dental offices in it. There was one irate phone call from, I think, a dentist who was apparently not a jazz fan. Less than a hundred people showed up. "It takes more that chill winds and lowering skies to faze Art Hodes," Lloyd Maffitt wrote in The Burlington Hawk Eye. "The 75 year-old pianist, born Nov. 14, 1904, in Nikoliev, Russia, and the sidemen with him comprising the Hot Three, played like it was indeed hot."

Diehard fans applauded the group "with near-freezing hands, photographed them and taped their music," Maffitt added. Hodes opened with a march, "so you can march around and get warm," and the men broke into "The Washington and Lee Swing." Art liked to say he was glad to receive requests but never played them. He broke this rule, though, playing "Tennessee Waltz" when someone asked for it. "If I'm laughing it's to keep from crying," Art joked at one point during the abbreviated concert.

I ruled the promotion "an artistic success" since, after all, it gave me an excuse to bring Art Hodes back to town. I've never had any regrets, except for picking bad weather. Justified or not, I took some pride in realizing that the Art Hodes who helped introduce my book was the same Art Hodes who made a splash at the Kool Jazz Festival at Carnegie Hall in June, 1981.

Some of the modern jazz players had laid an egg, it was reported in Variety. "It took Art Hodes to recapture the audience with a masterfully developed 'St. Louis Blues' prior to the introduction of 85-year-old Mama Yancey, a frail personage in a wheelchair who nevertheless put bite and emotion into her blues . . ."

On Sept. 13, 1982, Art wrote to say he had talked to Muse about the release date for a recording he did with bassist Milt Hinton after they played at Steamboat Days. The jazz veterans had hit it off wonderfully in Burlington the previous summer and did my favorite of all of Art's recordings, "Just the Two of Us," on Aug. 26, 1981. (It is Muse MR 5297 and includes such gems as "Willow Weep For Me" and "Miss Otis Regrets.")

"So my stay at the Mayfair Regent Hotel continues," the letter went on. "The place seems to be populated but by no means all Art H. listeners."

The Mayfair, an upscale hotel just off Lakeshore Drive in Chicago, gave Art a shot at playing an extended run at a grand piano in a ritzy room filled with Oriental vases, tapestries and other works of art. Millie and I went to hear him one night and it turned out to be one of the "small but appreciated" audiences jazzmen kid about.

I felt generous in the spring of 1985 and hired Art and his wife, Jan, an accomplished pianist who met Art when she decided to learn to play jazz, to perform at Southeastern Community College. It was a benefit for our local jazz club that was broadcast by Iowa Public Radio and attended by, I was happy to note, a SRO crowd.

"Hodes defined the blues," Maffitt wrote, "as something you feel. Not head music but heart music, and played his own composition, 'Plain Old Blues.'"

The program included "Muskrat Ramble," dedicated to Louis Armstrong, and "Didn't He Ramble." The styles of James P. Johnson, Fats Waller, Tatum and Morton were explored in a medley of their signature tunes. The Windy City was saluted with "Chicago," "Five-Feet-Two" and "Ain't She Sweet."

Art's former student, Jan, joined him for "After Hours Blues" and "Salute to Cow Cow." For a spiritual, they did "Just a Closer Walk With Thee." Art closed the concert with Gershwin's "Summertime" and, predictably, "When the Saints Go Marching In."

Compared with Oct. 2-3, 1980, this promotion was a howling success. Unfortunately, I didn't have a new book to promote. Also, I was a bit disappointed that the presentation of jazz history didn't interest the SCC students. Nearly everyone in the audience was middle-aged or beyond.

"No way and no words I'm about to express will picture my feelings about the date you provided us," Art wrote from his home at Park Forest, Ill., in a few days. "From the time we stepped into our room at the Holiday Inn where there was a basket of fruit. In the language of a musician, it was 'a gas.'"

May 14, 1985, Hodes was busy in Chicago as musical director when the Hull House Association honored Benny Goodman. It was on a Tuesday night, and I couldn't make it to the Marriott Hotel, but was glad to know Art was involved as BG received the first Hull House National Distinguished Service Award.

Bud Freeman was there, also, and described Goodman as "an absolute genius." Art recalled first meeting Goodman when Benny was about 11 years old and he was a teen-ager. "I was playing for a dance group," said Hodes, as quoted in the Chicago Sun-Times, "and the bandmaster asked if we minded if 'the kid' sat in with us. It was very impressive because he was already a good player."

Steamboat Days honored some of its originators on June 20, 1987. Hodes was the obvious choice to provide the music. He was accompanied by trumpeter Bobby Lewis and drummer Jerry Coleman, both from around Chicago.

There were about 400 people in attendance as the group played 20 tunes, including "Honeysuckle Rose," "Chimes Blues," "My Blue Heaven," "C Jam Blues," "China Boy," "Up a Lazy River" and, of course, "Just a Closer Walk With Thee." The turnout would have been better if the concert had been given more promotion. It got lost in the shuffle of other SBD activities, most of it having to do with country and rock bands. Art's combo was top-notch.

"A living legend returned to Burlington this weekend," Maffitt said in his review. "Hailed by New Yorker jazz writer Whitney Balliett as the finest living blues pianist, Hodes is or has been a columnist, radio personality and author. He has given countless lectures on jazz."

Art was looking forward to a concert tour around Cape Cod, at age 83, as well as trips to England and interior Europe. He had just cut an LP of Christmas tunes and one devoted to gospel music.

"I have great respect for Fats Waller," Hodes said in the story, "but also for Count Basie, Hoagy Carmichael and others who made important contributions."

Hodes told Maffitt some pianists stress technique at the expense of emotion. "They don't hold you. They're like authors whose technique gets in the way of the story. Technique alone doesn't hold you," he pointed out.

Millie and I were in Park Forest on Jan. 11, 1987, as Art assembled a combo to salute the tenth birthday anniversary of the town's Freedom Hall, an airy glass and brick theater devoted to the arts.

The group included trumpeter Warren Kime, trombonist Danny Williams, saxophonist George Dixon, bassist Duke

Groner and drummer Coleman along with Art and Jan at the piano.

It was a festive evening, with dinner served by a first-rate caterer, and the band was excellent. I especially enjoyed Dixon, who had played with Earl Hines around 1930, when he honked some profound blues on his alto. Kime offered a stirring "I Can't Get Started." Williams sang and played a fast and humorous "Someday You'll Be Sorry." Art and Jan did a rollicking "Pinetop's Boogie Woogie."

Sept. 4, 1988:

Barrett Deems, who admitted to being beyond 75 at the time, jokingly referred to them as "the over the hill gang." No one laughed, though, when Hodes, trumpeter Doc Cheatham, Bud Freeman and Deems sat down to play at the tenth annual Chicago Jazz Festival.

Billed as "the Swing Era All Stars," and joined by clarinetist Frank Chace and bassist Eddie DeHaas, the veterans were in a prime time slot as the weekend-long event neared its climax. It was, unfortunately, to be a rain-shortened gig in Grant Park.

There had been a threat of foul weather all day. "It's going to snow," Deems warned the Labor Day crowd as the musicians did their sound checks a few hours before the 6 p.m. show. Their first number: "At Sundown."

The combo sounded good, drawing cheers and applause from the some 50,000 jazz fans braving the sharp winds off nearby Lake Michigan, plus a mid-afternoon drizzle. Freeman, impressed by Cheatham's effervescent solo, followed up with a booming chorus. I recalled the 1938 session he did for Commodore with pianist Jess Stacy and drummer George Wettling. Bud had grown frail but the spirit was still in him.

Hodes, just back from a tiring tour of Scotland, was backed by Deems in a powerful "St. Louis Blues" that ended with him pounding at the keyboard. The crowd went wild.

Then it was Cheatham's turn to shine. He was featured on "I Want a Little Girl," a tune he did for years at Sweet

Basil. Doc had the crowd in his palm as he spoofed the lyrics: "Maybe I'm looking for a mother, not a girl, who can cook for me and sew . . ."

The rains came, at last, just as Doc was winding up "Little Girl." The musicians, with help from some frantic stagehands, moved the piano, drums and their other paraphernalia to the rear of the covered Petrillo bandshell. Out front, thousands of red, yellow, blue, black and tan umbrellas flew open as if on cue.

The rain stopped in 15 minutes. The band came back with vigor to do "Three Little Words," featuring Freeman's sax and Chace's hoarse clarinet. "He's a Pee Wee Russell clone," Hodes had told me before the performance.

The concert by Hodes and his men was much too brief. It had to end at 6:45 to keep the remainder of the night on schedule.

The Freedom Hall concerts became annual events and we attended them in 1989 and 1990, missing the one in '91 due to bad weather. I kept track of Art, who had developed a kidney problem that required him to carry a dialysis kit on the road, with letters and phone calls. He was getting some well-deserved "ink" in some of the jazz magazines and The Chicago Tribune. So I knew what he was up to.

"The overflow crowd that packed the Green Mill Jazz Club over the weekend heard something more than simply an evening of first-rate music," Howard Reich reported in The Tribune on Jan. 15, 1991.

"With 85-year-old Art Hodes at the piano and four excellent musicians at his side, Saturday evening's performance was more akin to an education in the origins of jazz and blues ... when Hodes plays a solo such as 'Black and Blue' you can hear early blues piano in its purest form ... younger players who render historic blues in percusive, barnstorming manner clearly miss the point."

Art returned to the Green Mill on Mar. 9, 1991. There was a "crushing" crowd, Reich noted, as "everyone wants to hear what the grand old pianist has to say."

There was another rave review for Art on Sept. 24, 1991, when he returned to the Green Mill. "Hodes can evoke this period (the twenties) as few others can," Reich noted. "Because he was witness to, and eventually participated in, the dawn of jazz in Chicago, his playing eloquently calls up that era."

Oct. 25, 1992, The Sunday Tribune devoted two pages in its arts section to Hodes, when his "Hot Man" book had been released after being in process nearly three years. "I was a lucky man to have lived in Chicago's jazz era," Art was quoted as saying. There was a very nice photo of him, full length, leaning against the grand piano in his home. He had suffered a stroke in January and wasn't able to play. It was apparent that his illnesses had taken a toll.

"Hot Man," co-written by educator Chad Hansen, is a candid story of Art's life. It includes mention of his years of hard drinking, which ended when he came back to Chicago from New York in 1950. But it is mostly a book about music. It tells, for instance, of when Art ran a jazz club with Pee Wee Russell, and of his friendships with Bunk Johnson and Sidney Bechet.

"Every hot man looked up to Wingy Manone.," Art wrote in his last jazz book. "He lived the music. Our apartment was like a who's who: Max Kaminsky, Danny Alvin, Krupa, Teschemacher, Red McKenzie, Wettling, Paul Mares. For me it was all school, only school was never like this. You awoke to music, and you were swinging all day. At night it was for real."

Mar. 4, 1993:

Jan, who had been wonderful for Art since their marriage in 1983, phoned to tell us about his death. We drove to the funeral on a cool, beautiful day.

A seven-piece band led by trombonist Jim Beebe broke into a spirited "Bye and Bye" minutes before the service began in the Calvary United Protestant Church, which was filled with musicians, neighbors and other friends.

The bandsmen, who had all played for Art in the Chicago area, included trumpeter Lewis, drummer Coleman, pianist Joe Johnson, trombonist Bill Hanck, clarinetist Franz Jackson and bassist Jimmy Johnson. One of Art's piano students sat in for a number.

Jackson sang "My Blue Heaven" in ebullient fashion, following a husky-toned solo. "Black and Blue" was next, with Jackson doing the vocal and Lewis piercing the air with a moving, high-note solo. The band, wailing in grand fashion as toes tapped throughout the church, followed up with "When the Saints Go Marching In," "A Closer Walk With Thee," "Tin Roof Blues" and, finally, "Amazing Grace."

"Art wants all of you to sing on this one," the pastor said when "Amazing Grace" was announced. There were tears from some of the mourners, then some laughter as several of them reminisced about Hodes.

"When I was a kid," Beebe recalled, "one of the first records I heard was a 78 on Blue Note that featured the Art Hodes band. I still remember every note of it."

Jackson remembered the leadership Art provided in integrating the Chicago union that had been split into black and white locals.

"He was a marvel," said Lewis. "Not only to play with but to listen to. And believe me, in the 32 years I was with him I never heard Art play a wrong note."

One elderly man told about taking his pesky grandson to Hodes for piano lessons. He learned that even when he appeared to be dozing Art could always recognize "just one sour note."

A woman said the night Hodes played "Sweet Georgia Brown" for her was a highlight of her life.

Nervously, a young man told what Art had done for him by way of non-musical guidance "when my life needed to be straightened out."

Later, I wrote to the IAJRC Journal and The West Coast Rag to urge contributions to a memorial for Art with the

Chicago Federation of Musicians. Then money is to be used to help perpetuate live music.

"I knew Art for 30 years and can attest that, along with his musical and writing virtues, he was a very honest and dependable man," I noted. "I booked him a year in advance for my retirement party in 1987. Art and his wife, Jan, drove nearly 500 miles to and from the party. I paid him a reasonable fee, of course.

"Afterwards, I found out that he could have played in Chicago that weekend for more money. It was a gig that was offered to him after he had agreed to play for me. A deal was a deal with Art. He'd never break his word."

On top of that, Art always arrived well in advance of his performance. I never saw him dash in and play without adequate preparation. He was there early to check out the piano, the sound system and, of course, "the gate."

He was a pro.

# John Bunch

Whenever a discussion of Benny Goodman's pianists comes up there's sure to be mention of Teddy Wilson, Jess Stacy and Mel Powell. Joe Bushkin and Johnny Guarnieri were among the Goodman greats. Count Basie recorded with BG's most celebrated Sextet. The star-studded list goes on and on. Hank Jones. Marian McPartland. Andre Previn. Jimmy Rowles.

But a very able, unpretentious pianoman named John Bunch could, I believe, rival Wilson in having logged the most keyboard duty with the King of Swing. His on-and-off tenure, which continued until weeks before Goodman's death, spanned 29 years.

"My first job with Benny was in 1957 when he put together what turned out to be his last fulltime band," John told me in 1993. "Urbie Green fronted the band on week nights while we did one-night stands and Benny led it on weekends. Rolf Kuhn, a German musician, played BG's parts when he was absent. This went on for about three months, the final part of the year."

I wasn't aware that John was with Goodman in 1957, thinking his first job with BG was on June 19,1960, when a crew that included Red Norvo, Flip Phillips, Jack Sheldon and Green appeared on Ed Sullivan's television show.

It was a test of Bunch's considerable skills when Benny's group ignited a rapid-fire rendition of "The World Is Waiting for the Sunrise" with guitarist Jimmy Wyble, bassist John

Mosher, drummer John Markham and Norvo along for the ride.

I saw the broadcast and was impressed by a lanky, unheralded (at least to me) pianist I would, in time get to know and hear play on a dozen or more occasions, even in a cocktail lounge while sailing the Caribbean.

I met John Bunch during the Labor Day weekend, in 1963, amid a whirlwind tour of jazz venues in New York City. I'd spent a week as a newsman on a VIP cruise aboard an aircraft carrier, the Lake Champlain, and was headed home from Rhode Island when I opted to stay downtown instead of at a motel near Idlewild.

In the space of five hours I heard Coleman Hawkins at the Village Vanguard, Stan Getz at Basin Street West and Gene Krupa, Charlie Ventura and Red Allen at the Metropole. I also saw Cootie Williams, Jonah Jones and Roy Eldridge that memorable night. I just about shot my wad on cab rides.

It was a Saturday and the Metropole was packed. Bunch was in the crowd, jammed near the bar with a couple of hundred other sardine-like jazz fans, and I recognized him.

He was eager to talk and told me he had been at the RCA studio a week earlier (Aug. 26 or 27, 1963) when Goodman, Wilson, Krupa and Lionel Hampton cut the sides for an LP titled "Together Again!" It was an "inspired" performance, Bunch declared. "I don't know what got into Benny but he was blowing his tail off, playing as great as ever."

Bunch was the big band pianist on Goodman's tour of Russia in 1962 when, according to reviews, some of his clarinet playing wasn't up to his standards. I had talked to trumpter Joe Newman about the USSR tour late in 1963. "We were pulling for Benny to do better," he said. The LP set from the tour, which is quite good, was the result of some editing, according to Newman.

The next time I saw Bunch to talk to was in 1985 when he was playing at Fat Tuesday's in New York. He was seated at the bar a half-hour before showtime and, once again, was very approachable. He was with Scott Hamilton's combo doing a show that featured a parade of such standards as "Drop Me Off In Harlem" and a nifty "Limehouse Blues."

My wife, Millie, became alarmed during the first set when she realized the diamond was missing from her ring. Our waitress got into the act and we were all just about going ballistic when Bunch arrived, during an intermission, with a flashlight (the club only has a few ten-watt bulbs in it) to help in the frantic search. "No extra charge for this," he quipped, or words to that effect. The diamond was discovered minutes later in Millie's handbag, where it had fallen when it came loose from the setting.

Bunch's style is comparable to Wilson's and, I suppose, that was a reason he worked for Goodman so much over the years. He is in a class with Jones or McPartland, in my opinion, and his credits include time with the bands of Woody Herman, Maynard Ferguson and Buddy Rich. So he's a swinger.

John was also Tony Bennett's musical director from 1966 to 1972 and wrote a lovely ballad, "It's Love In the Spring," that was praised by George T. Simon when he reviewed the "Jubilee" LP that Bunch did with guitarist Cal Collins and bassist George Mraz. (This session was produced by Gus Statiras in New York and was issued as Audiophile AP-184 in 1984).

Some of Bunch's performances with Goodman stick in my mind more than others, naturally enough.

It was on Oct. 29, 1977, at Stephens Auditorium in Ames, when Goodman came off the wall with a solo on "Poor Butterfly" that knocked everyone out, even the janitor if he was within earshot. Bunch plays with a light, but prodding, touch and I think BG benefited from his nudgings in that spectacular performance. He seemed lost for a while. When he found himself he beamed, glanced at the drummer and everyone in the combo reacted with elation.

Bunch was a key element, too, when he appeared with Goodman's combo at the first annual Chicago Jazz Festival on Sept. 2,1979. Mel Torme and Adam Makowicz were also on the program that Sunday night but Benny and his combo were the headliners.

I hadn't heard Goodman and Bunch do "Send In the Clowns," except on an LP, and was delighted at the marvelous job they did bringing the more than 75,000 people to an appreciative hush. "Bunch was fine as usual," I wrote in my notes. "Beautiful!"

During our conversation in '85 at Fat Tuesday's I had mentioned how hectic it is cabbing from one club to another to hear jazz in New York. "You should try a jazz cruise," he suggested. We took the first of our Caribbean jazz cruises, on the Seaward and later on the Norway, in 1988.

On the 1988 cruise, Bunch was among the players featured in a "piano spectacular" directed by Powell, who had been a teen-age sensation with Goodman in 1941-42. Each artist was allowed two tunes and John's numbers were Charlie Parker's "Au Privave" and, for a change of pace, Leonard Bernstein's seldom heard "Lucky to Be Me."

I taped the "spectacular," a term that made Powell cringe, and replayed it while writing this book. Bunch certainly held his own with Eddie Higgins, Dick Hyman, Norman Simmons, Dave McKenna and John Eaton. "It's an honor to follow John Bunch," Eaton said when he succeeded John at the piano.

"I'm really kind of shy about saying much when I'm on the stage," Bunch confided during the 1988 cruise. "It's something I probably ought to work on."

Bunch happens to be a self-contained sort of man, more than some of the jazz performers I've seen and known. But no more so than Wilson, Basie or Art Hodes were. Not everyone is meant to be a Fats Waller or Ray Charles.

Despite his man-of-few words demeanor, Bunch has been around the proverbial block as a musician and by way of his military duty. He was a bombardier in Europe during World War II and was a prisoner of war for several months, someone told me, after being shot down on his 17th mission.

I tried to get John to talk about his long-ago experience, mentioning that I had been a POW in Germany in 1944-45.

"The food was terrible," he groaned while making the kind of face a guy does when vomiting. Then he quickly changed the subject to something more appetizing, the Seaward's afternoon buffet.

"He was a weird guy," Bunch related when I asked him to recall his association with Goodman. "He fired me several times, just like that. But I'd always go back when he phoned. There was no way I could resist the sound of that clarinet."

Once, Bunch remembered, the enigmatic jazz legend began to offer him what seemed to be an apology. "He told me he realized he hadn't always treated me just right," John said. "Then in the next breath he asked what I thought we ought to play."

Goodman died a few months later. Bunch, at 72, was still playing the jazz circuit, mostly in the New York clubs so familiar to him, when this book went to press. It's a safe bet that each note he plays is, like my note to myself said 17 years ago, "fine as usual."

# Ellis Larkins

Ellis Larkins was playing a long, sleek piano at the Carnegie Tavern, on west 56th Street directly behind Carnegie Hall, wearing his usual tux.

It was early winter. Millie and I were in New York to shop, eat some deli meals, look around and hear some jazz. The music was the main thing and I knew what a beautiful pianist Ellis was from what I'd heard on records and read in Metronome, Down Beat, etc., over the years.

I took notes on Nov. 7, 1982, perhaps thinking that I might get around to doing a book on my jazz memories when the urge finally hit me. He did several brief sets and, as I noted in a column I wrote after getting back to Iowa, he played "like and angel" in his compelling style which, to me, sometimes has an eccentric halt to it. It always keeps swinging, after what seems to be some hesitation. This builds suspense in my mind as I listen to Ellis, wondering what he'll do next. It always comes out in gorgeous fashion with the melody Ellington, Gershwin or Harold Arlen wrote still intact.

That night, Ellis played "More Than You Know," "She Didn't Say Yes," "Honeysuckle Rose," "I Let a Song Go Out of My Heart," "I'm Beginning to See the Light," "Do Nothing Till You Hear From Me," "The C Jam Blues," "It Don't Mean a Thing If It Ain't Got That Swing," "Don't Get Around Much Anymore," "Prelude to a Kiss," "Just Squeeze Me," "Caravan," "Sophisticated Lady," "Things Ain't What They Used to Be" and, somewhere amid all the Ellingtonia, his deft interpretation of Bob Haggart's "What's New?"

I introduced myself to Ellis, pointing out I was merely a fan of his and not wanting to talk shop in a serious way. He proved to be a gentle-talking man with a sly sense of humor, sometimes expressed at they keyboard (but not often) by slapping one hand with the other if one of them had hit a wrong key.

We were in New York for a week and heard Fran Warren at Michael's Pub, Maynard Ferguson at the Bottom Line, the Jack Maheu combo at Eddie Condon's, a set by Sylvia Syms at Marty's the spirited piano of Dick Wellstood at Hanratty's, the Sy Oliver band at the Rainbow Room, Sarah Vaughan at Rodney Dangerfield's, the spanky Davis combo at Jimmy Ryan's and John Bunch at the Knickerbocker.

We also took in "Sophisticated Ladies," with Mercer Ellington's 20-piece orchestra. But I still wanted more by Ellis. So we went back to the Carnegie Tavern twice to hear more Ellington and also an Arlen medley that included two of my favorites, "When the Sun Comes Out" and "Blues In the Night."

When I wrote about Ellis playing "like an angel" I sent a copy to him so he would realize how much his music pleased me and, of course, my wife.

"Ellis thanks you for the lovely article," his wife, Crystal, wrote back to me within a few days. I had noted that he played 20-minute sets, which were brief compared with what Wellstood or Bunch might play.

"It was true that he played only 20 minutes during the period you mention," she said. "Normally, he plays 30 minutes then allows the waitresses to take time to get their checks paid. It allows customers to converse. Since he hasn't been well recently he found that he could not play with proper control longer than 20 minutes.

"Please do not let this keep you from visiting him in the future," Crystal added. "He won't always be ill."

Ellis was, in fact, robust and playing longer sets when we heard him at Spiaggia, a posh new Italian restaurant on Chicago's Magnificent Mile," on Apr. 28, 1984.

It was the same afternoon we saw Artie Shaw, about a mile away, and walked briskly to Spiaggia to get in on Ellis' first set.

He did an Ellington medley that evening, playing from an alcove located above and behind the bar. The music was great, despite a lot of chatter from the diners. I particularly enjoyed "Yesterdays," "The Very Thought of You," "If Dreams Come True," "I Want a Little Girl" and a laid-back treatment of "Sweet Lorraine."

We visited with Ellis, had a drink with him, took some pictures and met the man who financed the restaurant. I kept in touch with Ellis, via Crystal, and we were able to renew acquaintances in October, 1989, on the Seaward.

Ellis was on board to play in the ship's lounge, a task he undertook with relish, and to accompany Jane Harvey in a supper club format. This was an unusual treat, while cruising the Caribbean, and the pairing of Ellis and Jane was right down my alley.

The rolling sea, or something, bothered Ellis some on that cruise. But we got to do a lot of visiting and I heard him play some of my favorite tunes, including some seldom-heard ones such as "Please Give Me Something to Remember You By." I'm not sure I'd ever heard a jazz pianist do that tear-jerker before. Ellis did it with a characteristic lilt. It was either jazz or, as the Duke had told me, "just music."

Next to hearing him play, the best thing for fans of Ellis Larkins to do is read about his fascinating career.

"Years before Bobby Short became a cult figure," New York magazine reported in 1972," there was Ellis Larkins. He played piano for Ella Fitzgerald, Mabel Mercer and Joe Williams; he also coached and arranged, and led a trio." Then he retired, the article said, when rock 'n roll took over. But he made a comeback in the early seventies.

"Mr. Larkins is in a class by himself in the world of jazz pianists," John S. Wilson wrote in the New York Times, reporting on the long-running gig at the Carnegie Tavern. He played there, Wilson pointed out, "sitting ramrod straight, immaculately dressed in tuxedo and ruffled shirt, his huge hands, which span an octave and a half, moving over the keys with an exquisitely gentle touch." (The Carnegie Tavern engagement, which seemed to be made in heaven, lasted more than six years. "He finally quit," Crystal said in a letter, on Feb. 25, 1984, "after push had come to shove" with the club's manager).

Newsweek, recalling that Ellis had been "a child prodigy" in Baltimore, mentioned that he was trained at the Peabody Conservatory, as a teen-ager, then spent three years at Juilliard. At 19, he was playing jazz at Cafe Society Uptown.

Whitney Balliett, the New Yorker jazz writer who has long been fascinated by Ellis' mannerisms, termed him "a shy, brilliant, semitransparent pianist" who made his debut at age eight. His idols in classical music are Chopin, Mozart and Beethoven.

I've read that Ellis had idolized Fats Waller and Art Tatum among his influences. At one of the bars on the Seaward, I got him to talking about the jazzmen he had enjoyed and admired. Specifically, I mentioned Earl Hines.

"That's right," Ellis said, acknowledging that Hines had inspired him in the thirties. "But don't forget about Teddy Wilson!"

NOTE: Anyone restricted to just one Ellis Larkins recording should consider his CD, "Ellis Larkins at Maybeck," Concord Jazz CCD-4533, from a recital on Mar. 29, 1992).

# Dorothy Donegan

My awareness of Dorothy Donegan's awesome talent as a pianist dates back to 1946 when she had an afternoon program on WBBM in Chicago.

This recollection is memorable, in part, because my father, who seldom admitted enjoying my kind of music, had recommended Dorothy to me. Was he actually a closet jazz buff?

Her repertoire back then was, as nearly as I can recall, some standard tunes and light classics. An occasional etude or sonata, perhaps, and maybe some boogie. But mostly jazz.

I knew that Donegan was still playing over the years. She was mentioned in the trade journals and made a few LPs that were in the Chicago stores. But she didn't play the more popular clubs, as far as I knew, and the fine Tatumesque playing I'd heard in '46 was a distant memory.

Donegan's comeback, if that's the right term for someone who really wasn't gone, came during a jazz cruise on the Norway in the fall of 1990. "Her first performance was well-attended," producer Hank O'Neal reported, "but she startled an audience who knew little about her. The next evening it was impossible to get into her show; two days later people gave up their dinner to make certain they could find a seat."

I met Donegan on the Norway and was, along with everyone on board, fascinated by her off-the-wall humor as well as her amazing talent at the keyboard. Amazing isn't too strong a word for it.

She was booked for a Civic Music concert at Burlington in the fall of 1992 after I came home raving about her rare combination of musicianship and comedy, rivaling Fats Waller in this regard.

An article I wrote for The Burlington Hawk Eye, to plug the concert, noted that Donegan was born in Chicago in 1924, that she now lived in Los Angeles, and that she had been pegged by critics as "a bona fide jazz legend" and, predictably enough, "the queen of the eighty-eights."

Donegan began studying music at age five, I wrote, with inspiration from her guitar-playing mother, and went on to study under Rudolph Ganz at the Chicago Musical College. She was in a movie called "Sensations" and recorded for Decca, Victor, Roulette and Capitol while playing, without the kind of recognition she deserved, at such clubs as the Embers in New York and London House in Chicago.

My wife and I were "flabbergasted" by Donegan, I declared. One morning, after she had presented a tumultuous concert in the vessel's theater, Donegan received a standing ovation as she came to the dining room for breakfast. She responded with a few choruses of "Poor Butterfly" at the keyboard of a tired-looking upright used for sing-alongs on the Norway.

Musicians dig Dorothy as much as her fans do, I pointed out. It's not unusual to see a well-know jazzman in the wings with his eyes riveted on Donegan as she plays.

"Dorothy has always been exciting," Illinois Jacquet, one of her biggest fans, told me when he and Donegan were at the Sarasota Jazz Festival a few years ago. "One time in Paris she went into a boogie woogie thing and just about drove those people out of their minds." Donegan played with Jacquet's big band at Sarasota, with no rehearsal, and gave all of us the same degree of euphoria she had sparked in the crowd at the Meridien Hotel.

Whitney Balliett referred to Donegan in The New Yorker as "a virtuoso pianist, an electric performer and a transcendent clown." Her technique approaches that of Tatum, he wrote. "On fast numbers she swings as hard as any pianist who ever lived, and on slow ballads she is as delicate as a rose." This is strong praise from a writer known to mute his enthusiasm when so inclined.

Prior to her Burlington concert, my wife and I heard Donegan at the Wintergarden night club in Chicago. I kidded her about doing a "tough" review when she came to Burlington. Instead, this is what I wrote:

When oldtimers bat the breeze about the musical "good old days" at Burlington's Memorial Auditorium, they can add Dorothy Donegan's name to their list of Duke Ellington, Louis Armstrong and Lionel Hampton.

Donegan's trio and saxophonist Red Holloway pulled out all the stops (Sept. 30, 1992) in a concert for some 1,300 Civic Music devotees. It featured tasty jazz, along with lush ballads, touches of the classics and some flashes of brash humor.

The result wasn't just two hours of top-drawer music, the caliber everyone should have expected. It was also a small miracle in that Holloway had never played with Donegan, bassist John Burr and drummer Ray Mosca. They hadn't even rehearsed.

Also, it should be noted that Burr and Mosca came to Burlington in a plane too small to carry their instrumental bulk. They used a bass violin and drum kit borrowed from local musicians, and had to make some rather significant mid-afternoon adjustments.

Donegan played the auditorium's vintage Baldwin. She had no complaints and, in fact, sounded as great as she did last winter when I heard her on a new Steinway. Everything was "letter perfect," in other words, at Civic Music's opening event of the 1992-93 season.

Donegan opened with what she referred to as "an etude," a brief fling at the classics to, perhaps, acknowledge that many in the audience were high-brow music buffs. She quickly found a more familiar groove with "Here's That Rainy Day." Offering flurries of Oscar Peterson and Erroll Garner, mixed in with her own Doneganisms, as Burr eagerly plucked his bass and Mosca waved his brushes with aplomb.

"Lullaby of Birdland" was next, with interpolations of "Love Me or Leave Me" and, for a bonus, a dash of old-fashioned stride piano.

After that, there was a quick "history of jazz" in which Donegan took to the microphone to remind that it takes white and black keys to play "The Star Spangled Banner." She mentioned that jazz began in the bawdy houses around New Orleans, but that it progressed to be the nation's most outstanding native art form.

She played "The Entertainer" to illustrate the king of ragtime a boy might have played on a plantation. After that, Donegan romped through "September In the Rain" the way George Shearing did it in New York clubs and, as a tribute to Garner, a genius who was said to be unable to read music, she played his elegant "Misty" without variations.

"Time After Time" changed the pace a bit, with a vocal by Donegan that proved that she has dulcet pipes. She and her sidekicks shifted gears for an uptempo "Makin' Whoopee," as Burr strummed away at his bass and his boss hammered her elbows on the keyboard to add an ! to her hot licks.

Holloway entered at this point, carrying two saxes he had brought from Los Angeles, to join with Donegan's group, which had flown from Chicago after a week-long gig at Joe Segal's Jazz Showcase. He opened with Milt Jackson's "Bags Groove," a fast blues that was given a lift via Mosca's cowbells and Burr's bowing.

Holloway followed up with his husky, occasionally frantic, solo on tenor horn with a novelty number, "Benny's From Heaven," that might have been too risque for Civic Music as recently as the fifties or sixties. (It had to do with a GI who had been overseas three years and came home to find an infant son).

"Lover Man" was Holloway's next offering, on alto sax, and it was in a league with what any great altoist, such as Johnny Hodges or Willie Smith, might have done with the jazz-tinged ballad. How, I wondered, could they play this intricate number so flawlessly without even a warm-up?

Donegan was spotlighted in a gorgeous "My Funny Valentine," my pick for her high point of the evening, if any of her solos could be isolated for praise. She and Holloway then did a long-ago Count Basie number, "Cute." Dorothy devoted the next ten minutes to a dazzling medley that started with "But Beautiful" then drifted into some urgent blues, breathtaking boogie woogie and snatches of such standbys as "Hello Dolly," "Down By the Old Mill Stream" and "London Bridge Is Falling Down."

(It was break time and Donegan, a bit limp from all her pyrotechnics, headed off stage for a snack. I interviewed her a few minutes and asked her to autograph a photo my wife had taken of us at Sarasota. She was eating a sandwich with one hand while writing with the other. So I wound up with her thumb print as well as her signature on the photo's mat).

After being refreshed, Donegan opened the second part of her show with a medley that included "Green Dolphin Street," for the most part, amid an explosion of notes during which her hands were constant blurs. "Deep Purple" got into the act. So did "Three Blind Mice."

"Lover" was played with blinding speed, and became a 12-minute tour de force before Donegan was finished with it. Then the tempo as slowed, almost to a crawl, as she presented "Memory" with all the TLC any pianist could have mustered.

"Flight of the Bumblebee" proved to be calisthenics for Mosca and Burr," in tandem with Donegan. The threesome concocted another medley at this point, running the gamut from bits of the classics to "Old MacDonald's Farm." It wound up with "Bye Bye Blackbird" after a boogie treatment of "St. Louis Blues' and, to no one's surprise by this time, "Happy Birthday," "Matilda" and "Clair De Lune."

Holloway came back for a torrid "Love For Sale" that was played much, much faster than what Cole Porter had in mind. Donegan tickled the crowd with some sly lyrics to "As Time

Goes By." Then she added some inside humor imitating Rose Murhpy's tiny-voiced "I Can't Give You Anything But Love" and, among other vignettes, Della Reese's "Mean to Me," Pearl Bailey's "So Tired" and Billie Holiday's plaintive "He's Funny That Way."

The result was a concert that appeared to make everyone happy, including the most sophisticated ticketholders. It was, in my opinion, one of the finest jazz shows presented in Burlington during the past half-century.

# Peter Nero

When he played a Burlington Civic Music concert on Nov. 24, 1965, pianist Peter Nero got double coverage in The Hawk Eye. I did a pre-concert interview while Lloyd Maffitt covered the main event, pen and notebook in hand.

"Kids often ask me if they should go into music for a career," Nero told me the afternoon before his concert. "Usually, they ask that question because someone has advised them not to do it. No one would try to talk them out of being a doctor or an engineer. But it's always soul-searching time when a career decision involves music."

Nero, who was 31 at the time, said he told youths serious about music that the decision "is up to them." He also advised that "determination, not talent alone," holds the key to success in music.

"I tell them they have to decide what they want to be and then go out and do it," the former piano salesman declared. "It's not easy to become a good doctor or engineer any more than it's easy to be good at anything else. It's a fact that someone's being good doesn't necessarily mean he'll be appreciated."

Success in music can hinge on "politics," Nero added. He meant, of course, being able to open some doors by knowing "the right person."

Nero, whose keyboard style is a mixture of jazz and the classics, had just finished a practice session on the auditorium's grand piano, one he hadn't played. Much of the half-hour was spent doing scales, much as a novice might do them.

Then, with a plastic-tipped cigar in his lips, Nero threw his head back, grinned and broke into a sparkling rendition of "I Remember You."

"I always try to practice for 30 minutes or so before a concert to stay in shape," said Nero, a very calm and affable man. "A two-hour concert is a lot of playing."

Nero said he spends an hour or more at the piano each day when not on tour. "It all depends on how good a shape I'm in," he remarked.

The Juilliard-trained pianist, who was going to a symphony concert in Washington the next weekend, said he was looking forward to doing some composing. "But in this business you just don't make plans," he sighed. "There would be too much conflict right now if I took time out to write some movie scores."

Nero's jazz style reflects his classical regimen. But he "loves" hot music, he emphasized, considering Art Tatum to be "tops" at the jazz keyboard. "I idolized him," Nero reported. "But I don't exclude the other greats such as Oscar Peterson, Erroll Garner and Earl Hines. They're all wonderful performers."

After his concert, I added to my story, Nero was swamped backstage for 20 minutes by teen-agers wanting autographs and a chance to take pictures.

The pianist also drew raves from Hazel Witte, president of the Civic Music group. "I've never heard such stupendous arrangements," she exclaimed. "You can tell he's a Juilliard graduate. That sound is in everything he plays."

I had heard Nero in the Quad Cities the previous weekend and was tied up teaching a night school writing class the night he was in Burlington. Maffitt, a newsroom friend who specialized in reviews, filed this report:

"A suave character with a sophisticated sense of humor and a fantastic piano technique brought a couple of sidekicks to the auditorium last night, and the trio turned on an audience that filled the building to capacity.

"Peter Nero, drummer Joe Cusatis and bull-fiddler Barre Phillips deftly blended long-hair and crew-cut music in the manner made famous by the late blind pianist, Alec Templeton, opening their program with the old pop song, 'Button Up Your Overcoat,' as it might have been played by Mozart.

"This was followed by Cole Porter's 'Night and Day,' a la Beethoven.

"The threesome then rendered 'People' and followed it with a blend of 'Tea for Two' and the familiar Tchaikovsky theme that was popularized by Freddy Martin as 'Moon Love.'

"Phillips then got his moment of glory with a solo version of 'They Can't Take That Away From Me,' then the trio played a Porter medley. Nero, who quipped and commented throughout the show, confided that Porter had been one of his favorite composers. The medley consisted of 'Just One of Those Things,' 'Love For Sale,' 'True Love,' 'Every Time We Say Good-bye' and 'It's All Right With Me.'

"'Two Bass Hit, starring Cusatis in the most amazing display of percussion virtuosity ever seen in (Burlington), followed and the first half of the program ended with music from 'Porgy and Bess.'

"The second half began with tunes from 'My Fair Lady,' including 'Show Me,' followed by 'I Could Have Danced All Night' as Johann Strauss might have composed it.

"Then more Gershwin, "Someone to Watch Over Me,' and the folk song, 'Scarlet Ribbons.'

"Nero then played 'More In Love,' from the score of the movie, 'Sunday In New York,' composed by Peter Nero.

"The talented trio brought the program to a close with another Gershwin number, 'I Got Rhythm,' played as a series of variations, each representing the style of a composer, Mozart, Beethoven, Liszt and Rachmaninoff, and ending with a final variation on the Doublemint gum TV commercial."

For their encore, Maffitt reported, "the threesome kicked 'Over the Rainbow' all over the place."

# Freddy Cole

Nathaniel Adams Coles, who delighted millions as Nat "King" Cole, died of cancer in 1965 at age 48, I reminded readers of The Hawk Eye on Sept. 13, 1991.

But, I reported, his glittering style as a singer and pianist was on display in the Burlington Auditorium the previous night when Nat's younger brother, Freddy Cole, held some 1,200 people in his palm for 2 1/2 hours.

It was, my review related, pretty much an evening of Nat Cole's music under the broad-minded auspices of the Civic Music Association. It takes some daring, even an element of financial risk, to present a jazz-oriented program in a forum that has been largely dedicated to the classics for 50 years, I pointed out.

The crowd was elated by the music of Freddy Cole, who studied at Juilliard and has a Nat-like voice that is just about uncanny. He was aided by fleet-fingered guitarist Jerry Byrd and Delbert Felix, an unobtrusive bassist. They reeled off 36 numbers that ranged from bittersweet (an obscure Cole Porter ballad) to jazz ("Satin Doll") and included a "Christmas Song" that, Cole joked, was "the first in this year's holiday season."

Nat Cole was, of course, a superb jazz pianist before he became an "Unforgettable" vocalist. So it was fitting that Freddy, around 60 at the time, featured his piano work as much as his mellow pipes in the fast-moving program.

The opening number, "I Remember You," previewed the Nat Cole mannerisms that won the audience to Freddy's side in a few minutes. "Paper Moon," one of Nat's big hits, triggered applause in its opening bars. "Just Pretend," then "Walkin' My Baby Back Home," were in the familiar groove.

Next, a medley of "international" songs brought Freddy to the microphone for "Tenderly" and "Stardust," in the style of Bing or Frank, as shimmering notes from Byrd's guitar filled the arena. This kind of music is usually played in a cocktail lounge. But the auditorium seemed to get smaller as the concert went on, a tribute to Cole's prowess as an entertainer and musician.

Cole returned to the piano for a beautiful "Autumn Leaves," embellished by a flurry of chords from Byrd. The trio ended the segment with a rousing "Around the World."

Felix, who was under wraps most of the night, was spotlighted in a "Satin Doll" solo that proved he didn't just come to Iowa for the ride. He played very well as Cole cut loose with some jazz that could have been from Oscar Peterson's bag.

Cole hit his high point of the night, perhaps, by singing the best version of "Lush Life" I had heard anywhere. In New York, in Chicago or on the SS Norway.

There was humor, too, when Freddy sang "Home Fried Potatoes," an item that reminded me of Nat's "Frim Fram Sauce." The trio romped through "Let Yourself Go," with special lyrics for the women in the audience, and "I Just Found Out About Love and Like It."

After a brief "pause for a cause," the musicians came back for a more cerebral set. It began with Porter's "I love Paris," then shifted to a ballad that brought Noel Coward to mind. There was more Porter with "I'm In Love" and the more familiar "Can Can."

Back in the Nat Cole groove, Freddy offered up "The Best Man," "Route 66" and a chorus of "Straighten Up and Fly Right." How many times, I asked myself, have I heard that tune?

There were more ballads associated with Nat. "Somewhere Along the Way," "When I Fall In Love," "Sweet Lorraine," "Mona Lisa" and, of course, "Unforgettable." Not great music, perhaps, but heady stuff.

"I'm not my brother," Freddy declared at this point, "I'm me. I entertain my special way. If I sound like Nat what can I say? I'm not trying to fill nobody's shoes ..."

In fact, it was a tight-rope act Freddy performed in doing the music of his famous, beloved brother. He was, as Freddy asserted, "the King to young and old."

The concert given in Burlington by Freddy Cole proved him to be a remarkable talent, if not an immense one. The guy plays fine piano, with both hands, in an understated style that never slips into bad taste or cliches. Nat can't be doing all that for him.

Freddy's vocals seemed to be about as good as those of any of today's male performers except for Tony Bennett, Mel Torme, Joe Williams or "Blue Eyes" himself.

It was a very well-balanced show that never lagged. It sent many people home feeling good, I'm sure, with a greater apprcciation of laid-back jazz.

If anyone is to perpetuate the piano and vocal artistry of Nat Cole is should, more than anyone else, be his kid brother.

# George Coleman

George Coleman was playing piano at a roadhouse near Keokuk, Ia., the first time I heard him. He was a progressive musician, judged by Southeast Iowa standards a half-century ago, though I hardly realized it.

It was late in the summer of 1942, several months after I heard Leonard Brooks at "the P-I." I got into the Lakeshore club with some older guys who had heard about "the colored guy who plays hot piano."

The Lakeshore, located near the Mississippi River, was no country club. About all I remember is bouncing over a railroad track on a bumpy road and there we were. Being there was an exciting, risque experience at the time I was learning there was life beyond what I'd seen on the movie screens.

Coleman's own tune, "Immaterial," is the only number I recall him playing. It had a rhythm much different than I'd heard at home, where my mother "played by ear," or from her brother. My uncle, Bert Danielson, was good enough to play in a bar at Peoria, Ill., and did such tunes as "Twelfth Street Rag" with a light, impish touch. Lynda Bied played more heavily, but quite well, on numbers such as "Moonglow."

Coleman's "Immaterial" had a touch of boogie woogie in it. He leaned more toward Mary Lou Williams than Pete Johnson or Meade Lux Lewis. His tune had sly rhythm and suspense.

By the time I was in junior college, around 1947-49, George had a band at the area's most popular night club, Sunset Gardens, in Gulfport, Ill.

"How High the Moon" was the jazz anthem at this time. I insisted that George's band play it each time I went "across the river" to whoop it up, often a nightly ritual. George had a smooth technique, stroking the keyboard and very rarely hammering it. He could swing as well as many of the pianists I was hearing on records from the West Coast.

The band included a be-bop trumpeter, who called himself Wesley J. Westbrooks and wore dark glasses and a beret. Wesley was good, in the Dizzy Gillespie vein. But he was too often drowned out by the noise in the club. The Boston Pops would have had the same problem on a Saturday night.

Jimmy Green played robust trombone, much the way the guys were doing it in Stan Kenton's band. Steiner Jackson, an elderly gent, played tenor sax the old-fashioned way with a big tone and considerable heat.

Sam Bates, whose fulltime job was with a railroad crew, was an adequate drummer who usually kept good time. He was also a swell guy who, like me, logged a lot of time at Sunset's bar.

Sunset wasn't a jazz club to rank with Eddie Condon's. But the band played just about every night of the week and there were jam sessions Sunday afternoons. Pete Pemberton usually drove up from Keokuk with his tenor sax. He would leave it in his car until he had a few drinks and, finally, someone would beg him to get his "axe."

I have surprisingly clear memories of a Sunday when the band, with George at the piano, got carried away on "Sweet Georgia Brown" and refused to quit. Pete held his own, and then some, against a "pro" named Vito Price who was with a band Chubby Jackson had brought in for a two-week gig. Pete had his cheering section and, naturally, we figured he had "cut" the big city saxman in the battle.

Sunset had done a tremendous business during the war, when the ammunition plant near Burlington employed around 12,000 people. Money flowed, along with the booze. The club's owners could afford good entertainment, drawing trade from 40 or more miles. Our good fortune continued until around 1950 with such performers as Julia Lee doing shows.

George Coleman was the catalyst for many years. I recall getting him out of bed one morning, around 10 o'clock, and taking him to our home to play a couple of numbers for my mother. He played a ballad, not "How High the Moon." She responded with, I think, "Linda."

It was 30 years before I saw George play again. I had heard he was working at a restaurant near Kewanee, Ill., and went there with Millie. He looked about the same, only heavier, but had been forced into a rut of playing mostly commercial stuff.

George's audience at Waunee Farm liked Irish tunes and novelties, but he slipped in some ballads and show tunes when he could. I was happy for him later on when he got an open-ended arrangement at a beautiful new place called Jumer's that replaced the Sheraton Inn at Galesburg. The owners went all-out fixing the place up, with loads of antiques and a great-looking piano that must have been the best George ever played.

George was very popular at Jumer's through the seventies and eighties. He usually played Fridays and Saturdays with a combo that included a guitarist, a drummer and a clarinetist, Dale Rowen, who played for kicks and loved to do Goodman tunes.

They played a lot of pop stuff at Jumer's. But they also played a lot of jazz and did everything very well. George's technique was still intact and I enjoyed hearing him do show tunes such as "Blue Moon" and "It Never Entered My Mind."

I hesitated to request "How High the Moon," knowing it wouldn't be the same without his Sunset band. I wish I had asked him to do it "for old time's sake."

George had a fulltime job handling orders at an art supply dealer's in Galesburg. He was getting into his seventies and developed some health problems. So he wanted to play less at a time when the people running Jumer's wanted him to play more.

"They want me to play Sundays," he groaned the last time I saw him. He continued to play a couple of nights a week. Things were getting a bit tense, I assumed, as he got to playing now and then at a jazz club in the Quad Cities.

George died on Aug. 11, 1991. Millie and I got the bad news from a mutual friend. We wanted to go to the funeral but had to miss it because we had tickets for a plane trip that day.

We sent flowers, of course. We also sent a note to George's wife, Betty, telling her that George's music will mean very much to me as long as I live.

NOTE: Bassist Jackson did not know George Coleman over the years but remembered his duty tour at Sunset Gardens when I reminded him of it. "I talked to Vito on the phone a while back," he said. "He's living in Italy." Jackson couldn't recall how the Sunset booking came about. "It wasn't a place we'd heard of," he said in 1993.

Jim Manard, a longtime Burlington area jazz pianist, told me Jackson might have been booked by Red McKinley, who played tenor sax around the area during World War II and was later managing Sunset. Bookings in that era included Doc Evans, the Dixieland cornetist, who liked to sit out the intermissions reading poetry at the east end of the club's Olympic-length bar.

# Anita and Others

She appeared too young and slender for Anita O'Day. But the woman I saw in the lobby of the Blackstone Hotel resembled her. I knew it was Anita when I heard her voice. Not singing, but giving an unlucky guy a piece of her mind.

It was May 4, 1990. It was Friday noon and O'Day, the best of all jazz singers (though I have preferred Ella Fitzgerald and Peggy Lee on ballads) was checking in for a weekend at Joe Segal's Jazz Showcase. Then 70, she was back in Chicago, her hometown, to reinvent some melodies.

"She doesn't merely embellish a song," as Howard Reich noted in The Chicago Tribune. "She rewrites it, turning melodies upside down, stretching phrases long past the breaking point, tossing in nonsense words and sound-effects that confound expectations."

It was a kick just to be sitting at ringside, a few feet behind her pianist, to watch O'Day at work. There were five shows, all of them featuring her intimate, personalized versions of "You'd Be So Nice To Come Home To," "Street of Dreams," "Yesterdays" and, of course, "Let Me Off Uptown." There was always some variation in the phrasing, the delicate nuances or, perhaps, the tempo. There was more purring than shouting. Even the slowest numbers managed to swing.

O'Day brought a drink with her on the stand each show. It might have been a prop. Maybe it gave her a feeling of comfort to know a highball was handy. The only time I saw her gulp one in earnest was Sunday noon, when the crowd was the largest. She tossed it down, then mounted the stage and sang her you-know-what off.

There was, of course, notable instrumental support with Gordon Brisker on tenor sax and Chicago's Art Hoyle on trumpet with, in particular, a stylish, fat-toned solo on "Love For Sale" that knocked me out.

Rusty Jones, the drummer, aroused a bit of Anita's ire when he failed to read her mind on a tempo shift. "It's bump ta bump ta bump," she explained, patting on a piece of his drum kit. Rusty, who is no novice to various jazz rhythms, took it with what seemed to be a forced grin.

"Let Me Off Uptown" doesn't sound right to me without Roy Eldridge, who was on the famous Gene Krupa record in 1941. It was still a treat, though, with Brisker taking the trumpet breaks on his sax. Of the two numbers, I always preferred "Thanks For the Boogie Ride." So I was pleased when Anita came close with "Boogie Blues."

It has been my good fortune to see O'Day perform many times over the years. She always seemed to be in top form in Boston, New York and Chicago. The closest I ever saw anyone come to upstaging her was at Rick's Cafe, around 1980, when pianist Norman Simmons got carried away with a rhapsodic chorus on "My Funny Valentine." Overall, of course, it was her show, her applause.

In 1987, we had seats directly behind the pianist when O'Day was at Fat Tuesday's. The combo launched the opening set instrumentally with a limp rendition of "The Night Has a Thousand Eyes," a tune I don't happen to like. "That was a helluva poor opener," Anita snapped as she neared the stage. Harmony prevailed, however, by the time she sang her trademark, "Wave." She followed up with "They Can't Take That Away From Me," "S'Wonderful," Street of Dreams," "Boogie Blues" and "Let Me Off Uptown." It was an abbreviated set, it seemed to me. But she sang as well as ever, though she apparently wasn't in the best of moods.

Later that night, O'Day was very nice about it when a fan asked her to autograph the sleeve on one of her 78-rpm records., At Jazz Showcase, I had asked her to sign a copy of her impressive book, "High Times Hard Times," for my sister. She was happy to do it and eagerly posed with me as my wife snapped a couple of photos.

Anita had forgotten a tune called "Deliver Me to Tennessee," though it is in the discography in her book. But she is a genius, or close to it, and entitled to be forgetful. Within reason, I think, she has a right to scold a drummer or nip at a bellhop.

There are, naturally, memories of other thrushes, canaries and assorted girl singers kicking around in my mind.

Sylvia Syms, certainly one of the best, delighted us no end when we saw her at Marty's on the East Side in New York. It was around 1983 and we saw her a year later at Rick's Cafe.

Syms was know as "the world's greatest saloon singer," but Marty's was an upscale place. Still, her style on such arresting ballads as "I Thought About You" and "I've Got a Crush on You" emitted an intoxicating kind of glow. It's difficult at times to tell a bar from a lounge. I know "a dive" when I see one.

I only talked to Syms briefly, at Rick's Cafe, when she told me Marty's had been shuttered because the owner had, as she put it, done "something naughty." I was saddened to hear about her death at age 73 in May, 1992.

She was preparing to sing "My Shining Hour," a number identified with her husky, intimate delivery. We had heard her do it twice, with sensitive backing from Mike Abene at the piano.

Syms, a close friend of Frank Sinatra, had played Bloody Mary in "South Pacific" and more than a million copies were sold of her recording, "I Could Have Danced All Night." Yet she didn't attain the popularity of a Dinah Shore or a Linda Ronstadt. What's new?

Julie Wilson isn't a jazz singer, per se. But she has a marvelous voice of jazz proportion and puts on a great show. So I am glad to have seen her in 1985 and again the next year in the Oak Room of the Algonquin Hotel.

Wilson, who launched her show biz career as a $50 a week chorus girl at the Latin Quarter, did a Cole Porter show when Millie and I saw her the first time. She is a slender, striking woman who can deliver "Easy to Love" or "Just One of Those Things" better than just about anyone in the supper club realm.

She was doing Irving Berlin on May 22, 1986, when we were joined by Jane Harvey, a very talented club singer herself, in the Oak Room. I had forgotten how may popular songs Berlin had written, including some like "Blue Skies" that were usurped by jazzmen over the years. Wilson did a humorous "I Love A Piano," with accompanist Billy Roy, and included "Oh How I Hate to Get Up In the Morning" and "God Bless America" in her eclectic program.

Maxine Sullivan was singing at Fat Tuesday's in June, 1985, the night John Bunch helped search for the diamond from Millie's ring. We were impressed when she stopped briefly at our table en route to the bandstand and enjoyed her set.

It included "Surprise Party," "I've Got the World On a String," "Every Time," "A Hundred Years From Today," "You're a Lucky Guy," "Ain't Misbhavin'" and "Just One of Those Things." I'll always remember her for "Loch Lomond" and also for pausing to say hello.

Ruby Braff's cornet and Michael Moore's bass added to my pleasure the night in 1986 when Rosemary Clooney sang to us, and a few hundred others, at Michael's Pub. It was the first time I had seen Clooney since 1947 when she and her sister, Betty, were with Tony Pastor's band at the Oriental Theater in Chicago.

I didn't realize Braff was on the stage. When he blew a low, shimmering note from behind the curtain, it sounded as if Bix was in the house. And he was just warming up.

Clooney sang more like a jazz performer than ever before, allowing Braff and Moore, also a stellar performer, frequent solo breaks. She sang "Let's Take the Long Way Home," "Bewitched," "Sophisticated Lady," "My Shining Hour" and

"When October Comes," all delivered with simplicity and great warmth. No vocal gymnastics or gimmicks of any kind.

It was a similar treat to hear Alberta Hunter sing the blues at the Chicago Jazz Festival in 1982. She looked very attractive in her lavender gown and stopped the show before uttering a note. It's that way with "a legend."

Ella was at Basin Street West the first time I saw her, doing nightly shows with Stan Getz and a band led by Buddy Collette. I was in New York for two weeks, going to a seminar at Columbia University, and saw four or five of her shows. She was at Iowa City in 1975, accompanied by Tommy Flanagan and trumpeter Eldridge.

The best thing about Fitzgerald, one of my music-loving friends pointed out, is her "perfect pitch." Her scat singing always made me squirm. But she was unbeatable on something like "Once In a While," "Try a Little Tenderness" or my pal's favorite, "Rain." (These tunes and 27 others are on "30 by Ella," recorded with Benny Carter, Harry Edison and Georgie Auld on a Capitol LP, SN-16276, that was reissued a few years ago).

Sarah Vaughan was, as they say, "an acquired taste." I enjoyed her with the Boston Pops at Ames in 1976, subbing for an ailing Peggy Lee. She was much more impressive at Rodney Dangerfield's on a cold, windy night in 1982.

Vaughan benefited, I thought, from the more intimate surroundings with her five-star combo. At Ames, there was a huge ensemble augmented, believe it or not, by 50 brass players from campus ranks.

She couldn't have been in better form at Dangerfield's. Most of her program was either at medium or fast tempo and there was never a lag.

I had heard that Sarah knew how to handle a noisy, thoughtless crowd. That proved to be an understatement when, in the midst of a rapid-fire "When Your Lover Has Gone," everything stopped. It was "splat," as if a bike rider hit a brick wall.

Some young people had been chattering during the show, and kept at it after a warning. "All right," she demanded after the music stopped. "All right, say it. Say what you got to say. Get it all out. Say it!"

The noisemakers left, rather than risk a heave-ho from Rodney's bouncers.

Then the woman the rest of us had come to see picked up where she left off, without missing a beat; "When you're alone who cares for starry skies . . . at break of dawn there is no sunrise . . . boppa doppa dop . . . boppa doppa dop . . . when your lover has gone."

# Pearl Bailey

It was in 1988, I believe, that I met Pearl Bailey in Chicago, quite by accident.

My wife and I were shopping at the Water Tower Place, on North Michigan Avenue, when I ducked into the Rizzoli book store for refuge from the commotion. I did a double take when I saw a classy woman sitting on a low flight of steps while reading from a kindergarten book to some tots she didn't appear to be with.

I walked by her a couple of times, then asked: "Aren't you Pearl Bailey?" This was surely a better approach than asking if she "used to be" Pearl Bailey. Right?

Bailey hadn't made any records in recent years, to my knowledge, and hadn't been on TV or in the movies. So I was glad to realize she was doing all right and that, like her husband Louie Bellson, she was easy to approach.

She grinned and was very anxious to talk, even to a stranger in a busy store. "That's right," she replied when I asked, while groping for something to say, if she didn't sing with the Cootie Williams band "a few years ago."

I gave her one of my cards, after fumbling a while for it in my billfold. I had told her we were going on a jazz cruise in a few months and that we were looking forward to hearing "Louie" on the ship. I had met him in the late forties in the Quad Cities, where he was raised, when he played at the Horseshoe Club with Buddy DeFranco, John Simmons and others when the Tommy Dorsey band was on furlough.

"I'm going to be talking to Louie on the phone tonight," she said. "I'll tell him to look for you on the ship." She assumed I had some connection to the music business, I think. My cards only refer to me as a free lance writer. (I bought 500 of them in New York years ago when collecting cards from jazzmen and being asked for mine in return).

With the ice broken, I asked "Pearl" if she had any plans to be with Bellson, perhaps the next year, for a jazz cruise on the Seaward or Norway. "No way," she replied. "I wouldn't be there just for the trip, only if they wanted me to entertain. That's what I do."

There was more small talk as Bailey, attired in a stylish black outfit with some expensive-looking jewelry, turned pages for the excited youngsters.

I have heard that Pearl Bailey could be curt, based on an incident involving a stagehand. This was my only conversation with her and I couldn't imagine a warmer human being. But in a long career in show business she must have had some bad moments.

Around 1980, we had seen Louie and Pearl at the Aerie Crown Theater, then five stories below Rizzoli's. Bellson is a great drummer, arguably the best. But his wife stole the show that Sunday afternoon, at least for me, with her wonderful "Memories of You." I've never heard a more intimate delivery by anyone.

Ask me to take a guess and I'll venture that Pearl was as grand a person off stage as on. I saw the look in Louie's eyes when he talked about her. She was "real," I think, around the clock.

Bailey's mind was on her United Nations activities the day I met her. One reason I gave her a card was so she could mail me a copy of a speech she was going to deliver in the UN on behalf of needy children. It came in a few weeks along with a photo of "Pearlie Mae" at her delegate's desk.

I was saddened to hear on Aug. 17, 1990, that Bailey had died, at age 72, while recovering from knee surgery.

Bellson, who had been married to her for 38 years, told a reporter: "I've lost my best friend."

A few years earlier, I had talked to Bellson about Benny Goodman's death. "Pearl told me about it," he said. "We both felt bad about it, since he'd done so much for me."

When I saw him in January, 1991, during the jazzfest at Rockford, Ill., I told Louie how sorry I was about his loss.

He thanked me, saying he was "doing all right" while indicating that, in old vaudeville style, the show goes on.

I wondered if he might have recalled the couple of times I told him how fortunate he was to have someone so near to sing him a divine "Memories of You."

# Peggy Lee

It was a thrill to see Peggy Lee at the Chicago Theater in August, 1942.

Lee was my favorite, "thrush" in that era, partly because of her fabulous looks. She could sing, too, and I had bought several platters she had cut with Benny Goodman, who spotted something in her others missed. "The Way You Look Tonight." Winter Weather." "I Threw a Kiss In the Ocean." "Not Mine." "That Did It Marie." "All I Need Is You." And, of course, "Why Don't You Do Right?"

Miss Peggy Lee, as she's been known in recent years, was the most beautiful woman in the Free World that night, I was convinced.

She wore a clinging, shimmering white gown that was curvy in exactly the right places. When she sang "These Foolish Things Remind Me of You," a torch song that stopped the show in the midst of the band's flagwavers, a sailor in the front row leaped from his seat as if to climb onto the stage. "You came, you saw, you conquered me ..." That line was too much for him, obviously.

Lee laughed. Then she went on to sing such hits of hers as "Sunny Side of the Street" with a Sextet that featured trombonist Lou McGarity and her future husband, guitarist Dave Barbour.

The full band joined for "Why Don't You Do Right?" It was the same as my record, note for note, with a trumpeter punctuating the lyric with growls from the back row.

She had been getting some lumps from a few critics with Down Beat and Metronome at the time. But I thought Lee sounded great. To his credit, Goodman stuck with her as such sidemen as Mel Powell and Vido Musso helped her in a technical way.

Norma Deloris Egstrom, who became Peggy Lee after going into show biz, was born at Jamestown, N. Dak., in the spring of 1920. She was discovered by Goodman's wife, I've read, in 1941 while singing in a chic lounge in Chicago's Ambassador West Hotel. The tune that caught Benny's ear was, Lee recalled in her autobiography: "These Foolish Things."

Lee replaced Helen Forrest when she went to Artie Shaw's band, and the rest is musical history. It's hard, I think, to come up with another swing era vocalist who became more of a success than Peggy Lee. She was a hit in the movies, wrote some big songs such as "Manana" and has remained on top for more than a half-century.

I didn't get to meet Lee in my travels as a jazz buff. That's why I can't refer to her as "Peggy," with ease, while writing about her.

But I've remained a staunch fan of hers and have felt for her when I've read about her illnesses and broken marriages. I sent her a note once, in a Nevada hotel, but it was merely a "thanks for the memories" sort of thing.

In 1972, while at Lake Tahoe, it was my good fortune to catch two shows by Lee at the King's Castle, then with a "name" entertainment policy on the north shore. She was backed by Mike Melvoin's brassy orchestra. The audience gave its biggest hand to a hit tune of that period I haven't heard recently, "Raindrops Keep Falling On My Head." My favorite that night: "These Foolish Things."

Lee looked great at the King's Castle. But she was in some distress getting her breath. "It's the altitude," she explained. It wasn't bad enough to affect her delivery.

My wife and I attended two concerts by Lee in Chicago during the mid-seventies, one at the Palmer House and the other at a club near O'Hare Airport.

She was still in fine voice, probably better than in her early years. But her torch song modus operandi had been shifted from "These Foolish Things" to "I'll Be Seeing You," delivered the same simmering way. She also did an outstanding job on "I Could Write a Book" with Lee joining in the applause as the band's keyboard player went into a romp that made the audience gasp.

During the Palmer House performance a busboy dropped a huge tray of dishes just as Lee began her show-ending "I'll Be Seeing You." She winced a bit, then cooed right through the aftermath.

It had been a tough night. At the outset, as Lee came running on stage, she began "I Love Being Here With You" into a dead microphone.

That's why she's called "a survivor."

# Kay Starr

"They just loved it," said Kay Starr. "They wanted to eat us up with a spoon. I was absolutely thrilled."

Starr, who gained initial fame with Charlie Barnet's swing band in the forties, was on the phone in her Los Angeles home and I was doing an interview to plug her upcoming show, "Swinging With the Stars," at the Burlington Auditorium.

Starr was referring to the audience the first time the show went on the road with Buddy DeFranco, the Four Freshmen and the Woody Herman band.

I asked Starr if, after so many years of it, she had any trouble "getting up" for a performance a couple of thousand miles away from Southern California. "It's no problem at all," she said. "If anybody can't get themselves up for a performance before a big audience they shouldn't be in this business. I can hardly wait to get to Burlington. I can't wait to do my thing."

Starr, whose background is in jazz, pointed out that she is "not a jazz singer" these days. "I tell some stories with my music. I don't tell jokes, but I tell something about the background of my music. I've grown."

The reason she's still popular, Starr explained, is because she puts on a simple, honest presentation. "It's a matter of integrity to a great degree," she remarked. "You can't beat that."

Performing on stage "isn't easy," she went on. "It takes a lot of heart and a strong stomach. The public can be fickle, you know, so there's a lot of rejection that has to be dealt with."

Her favorite song? "It has to be "Wheel of Fortune," Starr said. "It belongs to me, though others do it. It's the song that built the home I live in and the song that gave me my position in life. Singing it fills my heart with joy."

I also phoned DeFranco, who was at home in Florida, and Bob Flanigan, of the Four Freshmen, at his place in Las Vegas.

"Burlington audiences always do a good job rolling out the welcome mat," DeFranco told me. He remembered bringing the Miller-style band to town for Steamboat Days, doing a job with Art Hodes and performing with Tommy Dorsey. "I can recall the big applause in your auditorium," he said. "That was when the Dorsey band featured the Sentimentalists and Ziggy Elman."

How was he holding up after so many years on the road? "I still enjoy the on-stage part of it," he said. "I could do without all the plane travel and living out of a suitcase so much of the time. But music is still my life."

He has no plans to retire, the veteran clarinetist added. "I won't quit until I reach the point that I just can't play up to par."

Flanigan, terming DeFranco "the greatest clarinet player ever," vowed that the Burlington audience would "get an earful" from the musical troupe. He promised that the Freshmen would do a new piece, "Sophisticated Suite," featuring the music of Duke Ellington. "There's still a market for good music," he remarked. "It's not all rap."

"It doesn't get much better than this," I wrote in a review published July 23,1991. "A 2 1/2 hour show of good old days music, for the most part, that started with a bang and kept getting better as it went along."

Starr drew the most applause when she belted out such old favorites of hers as "Rock 'n Roll Waltz" and, of course,

"Wheel of Fortune." DeFranco proved to be the awesome player he is said to be on clarinet. The Four Freshmen sparkled with their horns as well as their singing. And the Herman band, ably led by Frank Tiberi, did a top-notch job all night with its own features and backing the other "stars."

Herman's theme, "Blue Flame," opened the concert and was followed by a roaring "Apple Honey," one of the flag-wavers from Woody's 1945 book. The 15-piece orchestra, including an eight-member brass section, then featured its saxes on "Four Brothers," followed by a lush "Early Autumn" with Tiberi doing the tenor sax solo made famous by the late Stan Getz.

After a Latin-tinged change of pace, featuring Tiberi's soprano sax and an unusual blend of baritone sax with one of the band's trumpeters, the band found its most familiar groove on "Woodchopper's Ball."

"Woody Herman is gone," I noted, "and so are such celebrated Herman greats as Zoot Sims, Bill Harris and Dave Tough. But today's version of the Herman band is an extremely good outfit with an abundance of spirit and fine musicianship."

The Four Freshmen came as close as anyone could expect in sounding like the combo that gained fame with Stan Kenton during campus tours, three decades ago.

"The Song Is You" opened their segment, with Flanigan playing trombone in the Kenton style and his cohorts making all the right sounds on trumpet, fluegelhorn and alto sax. "After You", with Flanigan joining the Herman section for a trombone choir, came close to genuine Kentonia. "There'll Never Be Another You" was in the same vein. "Laura" was dedicated to Herman's memory.

The Ellington medley included snatches of ten of the Duke's hits, with "Satin Doll" and "Solitude" drawing the most applause. There was a smooth transition from tune to tune, reflecting notable professionalism on the part of the quartet.

After intermission, DeFranco took his clarinet onto the auditorium stage for the third time since 1947. "He seems to improve with age," I reported. "He is a modernist to a considerable degree, with his awesome technique tending to overshadow his mellow tone."

During a Gershwin medley, Buddy exploded with a dazzling display of his virtuosity, notes on top of notes in the bop idiom. It was a blend of classics and jazz. That's the way the composer was headed when he penned "Bess You Is My Woman" more than 60 years ago.

With solid backing from the Herman crew, DeFranco earned ripples of applause with "Yesterdays," "More Than You Know" and Henry Mancini's "Mr. Lucky," a favorite of Buddy's that he played in Burlington with his Glenn Miller band in 1966.

Starr, who bubbled the entire half-hour she was on stage, sounded terrific and looked great. "She has a lot of pride," Flanigan had told me over the phone, "and it shows."

She launched her parade of hits with "I Love Being Here With You." Starr went on to give everyone something with an old song, "You've Gotta See Your Mama Tonight," a country tune, "Crazy," a jazz evergreen. "Honeysuckle Rose," a flaming "Great Balls of Fire" and then, with the band roaring into a Dixieland mode, a rousing "Bonaparte's Retreat."

The durable songstress saved her biggest hit, "Wheel of fortune," to end the show, grinding it out the way she first did it for Capitol on a 78-rpm platter.

The crowd of nearly 1,000 went wild.

NOTE: When I interviewed Starr I promised I would send her a copy of my review. She responded in a week or so with this hand-written note: "What a great surprise to finally get home and have your letter waiting for me. Imagine, someone keeping his word. It is most unusual and I thank you !!! The write up, of course, is what one always hopes to read and it has raised my spirits no end. Again, I thank you."

# *Travelogue and Essays*

# The Windy City

There was, once upon a time, a carnival sort of glow in downtown Chicago, the bustling area known as "the Loop." Especially at night.

It was that way, as vibrant as Place Pigalle, in the summer of 1945 when, at some risk to my eardrums, I spent an evening in the Garrick Stage Bar.

The Garrick, nested in the theater district on Randolph near Clark, was typical of many big city jazz clubs during World War II. It was an era of servicemen "out on the town" with civilians rushing to buy them drinks. There was, as I recall it, a guy on the sidewalk in front of the Garrick yelling like a sideshow barker: "No cover charge! The hottest jazz in town! The show starts in two minutes!"

I didn't need the hard sell. Red Allen and J. C. Higginbotham were on the bandstand that hot, humid, long-ago night, along with an underrated altoman named Don Stovall. The band was as good as I could have expected anywhere, even on 52nd Street or in "the Village."

The Garrick was a small place. It was, of course, dimly-lit with all the trappings needed to qualify it as "a joint." It was before air conditioning and, I believe, ventilated by a few electric fans. My memories of the jazz are more distinct, even after 49 years.

I was seated up front with a pal and warned him to be ready to duck from the slide on Higginbotham's trombone.

Allen was still in top form with his trumpet, at age 37, and playing the jazz warhorses he'd help popularize. "Good deal," he'd chant," while clapping his hands, with his horn tucked under one arm, his eyes closed while Higginbotham and Stovall delivered their blistering solos.

Several drinks had been consumed at our table, about the size of a Coke tray, by the time Red's show was going full blast. I remember him doing a hard-charging "Ride Red Ride," sparked by the hottest sliphorn smears I'd ever heard. But it was the band's current hit, "Get the Mop," that really rang my chimes.

There wasn't much of a tune to it and the lyric, such as it was, didn't make sense. It was around the time of V-J Day, though. The booze was flowing, happy days were here again and it didn't take much to amuse a rifleman just home from Europe and having the time of his life.

I was on Randolph Street last fall and walked by a parking lot where the Garrick Stage Bar was humming a half-century ago. The whole neighborhood has changed, naturally enough, with the glitzy State of Illinois Center where the Sherman was in the era when swing bands presided in the Panther Room.

The Capitol Lounge, across the alley from the Chicago Theater, where the big bands also played, is now a Foot Locker shop. I remember when Cootie Williams played there with his combo, four or five guys and all their paraphernalia crammed onto the back bar. He'd give the jazz fans a treat, maybe "West End Blues" or "G-Man," then do a novelty number such as "Talk a Little Trash." It all gave me a kick but Cootie had been so great with Ellington and BG that his lounge routine made his pre-war stuff a tough act to follow.

The London House, on Wacker Drive near North Michigan Avenue, which later became a budget eatery, featured many of the jazz world's most celebrated pianists in the fifties, and also some brassy bands. Maynard Ferguson played there and so did Allen, without Higginbotham but still loud enough. I saw Erroll Garner there around 1956, sitting on a phone book atop his piano bench while pumping new life into such evergreens as "Lover" and "Poor Butterfly."

The Blue Note, on North Clark Street, booked such top draws as Benny Goodman's combo and Duke Ellington's full band. Slim Gaillard, who had cut a jive-talking swath with bassist Slam Stewart as Slim & Slam in the swing era, headed the bill one night when I dropped in with some guys after a ballgame at Wrigley Field. Slim could play real jazz but he was into comedy, playing some choruses with his hands upside down, singing some "vouty" songs, etc. "Ah," he quipped after downing a green-colored drink, "Air Wick!"

Jazz isn't what is was in and near downtown Chicago. But hot music has survived there over the years thanks to some nick-of-time transfusions from such oases as Rick's Cafe in the Holiday Inn on Lakeshore Drive, about a mile north of the Loop.

My wife and I drove to Chicago four or five times a year in the late seventies and early eighties. We'd shop at Marshall Field's and have some deli lunches but our main attraction was Rick's. We've never regretted the 450-mile round-trips, even those when Hwy. 80 was packed with snow. Rick's was very dark, not just dimly-lit. There was a lifesize cutout of Humphrey Bogart at the entrance and the club's greeter sported a white jacket like the one Bogie wore in "Casablanca."

Tables were arranged so there were good sight-lines to watch such jazz greats as Oscar Peterson, Louie Bellson, Red Norvo, Zoot Sims, Al Cohn, Branford Marsalis, Joe Pass, Dave McKenna and Charlie Byrd.

Rick's also brought in such premiere vocalists as Joe Williams, Billy Eckstine, Helen Forrest, Chris Connor and Sylvia Syms. Williams, crooning "Autumn Leaves with no backing at all, was a performance to remember one October. It was Easter weekend, around the mid-seventies, when Byrd did a medley of "I'm Putting All My Eggs In One Basket" and "Easter Parade." We were in the front row and I gained some appreciation for an unamplified guitar.

Rick's went dark when the hotel became a Day's Inn and, I was told, the new owners opted not to subsidize jazz the way the Holiday Inn had done it. "You can't have big name stuff without some subsidy," a hotel staffer told me. The last time I looked the room that had been Rick's Cafe was a drab dining room with card tables and folding chairs where the attractive booths and glistening grand piano had been.

Joe Segal's popular Jazz Showcase, which had been on the neon strip called Rush Street, moved to the Blackstone Hotel, at South Michigan and Balbo, in 1980. Joe has done a fine job, considering that jazz has seen better times, with top-flight fare.

Jazz Showcase is in rather dignified surroundings. The room reflects the era when Dwight Eisenhower was among the hotel's guests. The club itself holds 200 or so music lovers who, over the years, have benefited from a superior sound system and a piano that has sounded better than it looked. The tariff is reasonable, usually around $10 per show. The cocktail waitresses don't twist a patron's arm (the way their forerunners did at the late, lamented Garrick).

Segal leans to modernists, as a rule, including Lee Konitz, Roy Hargrove and Elvin Jones, Dorothy Donegan and Ahmad Jamal are among the middle-road performers who've been in for week-long gigs in recent years. Big band fans have been treated to Akiyoshi-Tabackin and, on occasion, Bellson sitting in with the celebrated Northern Illinois University band led by Ron Modell.

My fond memories of Jazz Showcase go on and on, like Illinois Jacquet doing "Flying Home." There was the night, for instance, when a legend named Jabbo Smith, who had been forgotten by many jazz buffs, was brought in by sleeves-up pianist Art Hodes.

Jabbo had suffered a stroke, however. He couldn't play trumpet, to Art's dismay. So he sang "Sweet Lorraine," just the way a fabled jazzman should have done it. Then, to the surprise of everyone, he came off the wall with some gutsy blasts from a valve trombone. It added up to a precious moment in jazz on, to be exact about it, Oct. 8, 1983.

Von Freeman, the longtime Chicago tenorman, preached a 15-minute sermon one night after the Jazz Festival, chorus after chorus of a hardnosed "Lester Leaps In."

I heard Ferguson play "Night in Tunisia" five times one weekend at Jazz Showcase, and still wanted more. His nine-member crew also played "But Beautiful," but gorgeously. The sound approached a performance by Stan Kenton's big band.

Claudio Roditi, the fine Brazilian trumpeter, went to the piano once at the Showcase and pecked out a one-finger solo that captured the subtle swing of Count Basie. Toshiko Akiyoshi played a piano solo on "No Moon at All," while seated on a phone book the way Garner did it, that just about went into space.

The walls at Jazz Showcase have survived tremors from the brass of some of the most notable big bands. Other times, such as when Pass did "Feelings," the thrills were so muted I could hear ice tinkling at the bar.

Andy's Jazz Club, at 11 East Hubbard, is carrying on the city's tradition with, for the most part, local talent.

Andy's offers daily jazz from noon to 2:30 and evening shows starting around 5:30 p.m. The cover charge is around $4, or less. The kitchen serves $8 entrees. It's a blue collar place, though some jazz fans dressed up like the "swells" in Peter Arno's cartoons might drop in.

In the fall of 1993 the lineup one afternoon at Andy's included an emphatic pianist, Max Hook, with gifted bassist John Whitfield, who can rattle the glasses on the back bar. Their set, with only a half-dozen people to hear it, was highlighted by a glossy "What's New?" that rivaled any piano-bass duo in the business.

Bobby Lewis, a trumpeter with some Berigan in his ballad tones, and Barrett Deems, "the world's fastest drummer," were on deck that night. Dave Remington played some solid piano another afternoon, as a solo act. The evening show featured talented reedman Eric Schneider, who recalled his stint with Earl Hines via a fine alto solo on "Sweet Lorraine." The tune was, he reminded me, "one of Earl's favorites."

Jazz has been staging a comeback in the Windy City. Much of the rebirth is beyond downtown. Some of it is 20 miles north at Ravinia where, until a few years ago, jazz was only an occasional treat rather than an annual festival.

Chicago isn't the best place to find Dixieland. The jazz tends to be progressive, especially during the free Labor Day weekend extravaganza.

That is natural enough, I think. It was that way in the twenties when Bud Freeman, Frank Teschemacher, Dave Tough and others inspired a Chicago style that, to me, picked up where the "moldy figs" left off.

# Eddie Condon's

They played taps to end a great era in music when Eddie Condon's jazz club was shuttered on Aug. 1, 1985.

It was the best place of its kind in New York City, I am convinced, because of its location, on 54th Street near Seventh Avenue, and because the music was always so good. The bands started playing around 8:30 p.m., and kept at it with only a few intermissions until around 3 o'clock. It wasn't a "clip joint,' though the drinks weren't cheap.

Condon's was the victim of the wrecking ball, so another high-rise could be built in Manhattan. They should have built the insurance building, or whatever it was, around the club and kept it as a memento of better times.

It was my good fortune to be at Condon's several times in 1985, soaking up what was left of the atmosphere. I can attest that the club flamed-out in a style Condon himself would have appreciated. Top-notch jazzmen dropped in almost nightly to sit in with the very able house band. One evening in late June, Billy Butterfield shook off a bad cold to play a low register solo on "What's New?" that was a work of art.

There were some Wednesday afternoon jam sessions that summer. It was on June 26, 1985, when Leonard Feather dropped in and played piano, extremely well, as fellow critic George T. Simon played drums. Earle Warren, the ex-Basieite, was on hand with his alto sax. Jerry Jerome was there playing tenor, even better than he did in the forties. John Bunch was at the piano, representing the house, with an occasional lift from Bobby Pratt, who normally played trombone in Condon's band but was also a thinking man's pianist. Wayne Andre, who was on the Goodman band that toured Russia in 1962, was the trombonist.

Ali Reyerson was there playing flute and, to my delight, a dazzling Jane Harvey belted out a great rendition of "Them There Eyes." Jane had been a favorite of mine with BG in 1945. She had to be around 60, but appeared half that age in a sporty outfit with a huge, stylish hat.

Millie and I were at Carnegie Hall for the New York Jazz Festival's "Spanish Night" on June 22, 1985. I enjoyed the awesome technique of pianist Tete Montoliu, especially his lovely renderings of "Come Sunday" and "Lush Life." But the second part of the show, devoted to fusion, rock and flamenco numbers, simply wasn't jazz.

So we left, as quietly as we could, and walked three blocks to Condon's. Al Grey was the night's guest, playing with saxman Joe Temperley and clarinetist Joe Muryani. Grey was blowing with his customary drive and Pratt, rather than make it a sliphorn duet, was presiding at "the ivory crate." Jazz belongs in a "joint" such as Condon's, of course, more than in a concert hall.

Condon, a guitarist and wit, had died in 1973. The club at 144 West 54th Street was opened in 1975 by jazzmen Red Balaban and Ed Polcer. Their policy included no cover charge, a $7.50 minimum and, most important, a steady flow of music that leaned toward Dixieland, while avoiding the kind of stuff associated with high button shoes. The best word for it, probably, was "mainstream."

The club wasn't plush. It was just four walls, with a bandstand at the center of the west wall, just beyond a well-stocked bar. There were booths along the opposite wall, to the left as a customer entered the place. Most of the jazz fans sat at the small tables jammed together in the middle of the club. The restrooms were downstairs, where a guy could still hear the "thump, thump, thump" from the bandstand.

Most anyone, including some celebrities, might be at Condon's any night. Many of the habitues were foreign, including two well-dressed Finns next to our table the night Butterfield did his "What's New?". The guys, in NYC on business, bought the band a round of drinks and were staggered a bit by the tab. I joked about the drinks being "unaffordable" when purchased six at a time. "They're affordable," one of the Finns remarked. "Just unreasonable." But he got his money's worth.

Advanced amateurs played at Condon's on occasion. One of them, a dentist, played clarinet in a way that reminded me of Joe Marsala or, perhaps, Clarence Hutchenrider. (Hutchenrider was playing next door at Jimmy Ryan's one night, along with Max Kaminsky, when we dropped in around 1980).

I got acquainted with Dr. Robert S. Litwak, a professor of surgery at the Mount Sinai Medical Center, who loved to play drums at Condon's to unwind. He seemed ample to the task and would have been a handy guy if any of us had suffered a coronary or, more likely, taken a spill down the restroom steps.

Dr. Litwak wrote "a coda" for Condon's that appeared on the op-ed page of the New York Times, after playing drums at the club on its last night.

"On that evening," he related, "Condon's was jammed with aficionados who, hearing such fine music, could only shake their heads in numb disbelief that all of this was to become only a memory in a matter of hours."

Chairs and tables were stacked one on top of the other, Litwak reported, "oddly bringing to mind an image of coffins awaiting shipment. The bandstand was bare save for a plaintively silent piano, which had know the greatest of jazz artists in happier times."

Jazz is becoming "a threatened species," Litwak feared, as New York becomes a standardized city filled with lucrative skyscrapers. "Midtown jazz is gone. What will be next?"

The Des Moines Register carried a lengthy obituary for Condon's in which the writer, William E. Geist, bemoaned the loss of "the jazz club extraordinaire." He quoted a waitress, Toby Slotnik, as saying: "My customers are so upset that they're actually out looking for another location for us."

Recalling an earlier Condon era, The Chicago Tribune joined in the coast-to-coast wake by reminding its readers of Eddie's cure for a hangover: "The juice of two quarts of whiskey."

It was, by the way, Condon's habit to pin nicknames on those around his "joint." The guy who cleaned the toilets, for instance, was "Flush Gordon."

In 1993, it was obvious that New York was still an awfully busy place without Eddie Condon's. The traffic, the noise and the jammed sidewalks were the same. But I'm not sure it was really the same place.

The crowd from Condon's had scattered to other clubs, such as Jimmy Walker's on East 55th where a semi-pro band led by saxman Bill Simon played until he fled to the warmth, sunshine and geriatric jazz in Florida.

I read about a new place called Condon's. But it wasn't Eddie Condon's, I was told, and had little in common with the place Dr. Litwak and the rest of us loved.

It's gone, as the saying went, but not forgotten. The kind of place a jazz fan could write a book about.

# Sweet Basil

"Wynton Marsalis is here!"

The hostess at Sweet Basil was spreading the word as we stepped into the club, which was packed to overflowing, on Sunday, Aug. 7, 1988.

"So is Duke Ellington's sister, Ruth," we learned as we plowed our way into the mass to find two seats, settling down in front of the bandstand where some people don't like to sit.

Harry Edison was there, also, though his presence wasn't stirring any fanfare of Marsalis proportion. Sweets was in a booth talking to Marsalis as jazz veteran Doc Cheatham, the reason we'd gone to the club, weaved his way through such oldies as "Sweet Lorraine" and "Emaline."

Doc added Fats Waller's "I've Got a Feeling I'm Falling," and it was obvious the hornman, then 83, hadn't lost a thing in his technique the past three years. Not even Roy Eldridge, Hot Lips Page or even King Louis himself could top Cheatham when it comes to doing a lyric in intimate fashion. Red Allen was more boisterous. Ray Nance more hip.

"We've got something special for you," Doc announced around 3:30 p.m. "We've got Wynton Marsalis!" He also reported that Edison was nearby. But that name got lost in the chatter.

Edison led off as the threesome, accompanied by pianist Chuck Folds, bassist Bucky Calabrese and drummer Jackie Williams, began with "Just Friends." It was a fast ride. One spirited chorus after another as the trumpeters swapped licks for about 15 minutes.

Next, the trio glided through "Love Me Or Leave Me" at a Saratoga trot. Cheatham played in short bursts, making clear and concise statements that summarized his 60-year career. Marsalis, as expected, came up with flurries of awesome technique. Edison, showing the most power of the three, played with typical good taste and stirred memories of Jazz at the Philharmonic.

Edison retired to his booth as Cheatham and Marsalis combined on "Embraceable You." The audience calmed to a hush as the Gershwin standard flowed to an insinuating beat.

Sweets returned, refreshed for battle, for a brilliant "Sweet Georgia Brown" in which he and Marsalis got into a polite cutting contest. No rancor was implied, but the two virtuosos laid it on the line for a jazz-wise audience. Edison relied on his driving tone, while Marsalis flashed the ornate style that catapulted him to fame in the jazz and classical realms.

Cheatham had been playing 90 minutes before Edison, who was 73, and the younger Marsalis arrived on the stage. But he held his own.

Doc went on to do another set consisting of such tunes as Kid Ory's "Muskrat Ramble," "Love You Madly" and Waller's sly "Rump Steak Serenade."

Per his custom, the legendary Doc closed with his signature, "I Guess I'll Get the Papers and Go Home." He disappeared into the crowd and, I guess, got his papers and went home.

Aug. 8, 1993:

It is still possible, my wife and I learned, to have a good time in the Big Apple for less than a hundred bucks.

We spent $91, to be exact, for a good meal and some exciting jazz at two clubs, including transportation.

The tab included $7 for round-trip bus fare from New Jersey, $20 for three cab rides, $40 for lunch and entertainment at the Red Blazer, and $24 for two drinks, dessert and music at Sweet Basil.

We were staying across the Hudson River from Manhattan in Teaneck, attending a convention of the International Association of Jazz Record Collectors, referred to as IAJRC to make it fit on a logo.

It was only a 20-minute ride from the Marriott Glenpointe Hotel to the Port Authority bus depot on Eighth Avenue. We took a cab to the Red Blazer, where Sol Yaged has played

Sunday shows for many years. He's the guy who taught Steve Allen how to finger a licorice stick, but not how to act, for "The Benny Goodman Story."

Sweet Basil, on Seventh Avenue at the edge of Greenwich Village, is several miles - about 55 blocks - from the Red Blazer. New York can be especially nice on a Sunday afternoon and we enjoyed such sights as Madison Square Garden, a couple of fender-benders, and the hotel that, in the forties, was the inspiration for Glenn Miller's "Pennsylvania Six Five Thousand."

I've made no secret in this book, or elsewhere, of being a Doc Cheatham fan. He was 88 last summer but still good enough to be in demand on cruises and at festivals from coast to coast.

I think Doc has been one of the most spellbinding performers in jazz.

When he does a number such as "Let's Do it," for example, Doc can ramble on about having played it behind Billie Holiday. When he plays "Was It a Dream?" he can explain that it is a rarity, a jazz waltz, written for a cabaret singer in New Orleans where, in 1925, he played in the floor show band. ("Was It a Dream?" is among the 14 excellent performances on Doc's latest record, "The Eighty-Seven Years of Doc Cheatham," available on Columbia CK 53215).

Folds, Calabrese and Eddie Locke, who drummed with such greats as Coleman Hawkins, were backing Cheatham the afternoon of our too-brief visit among the canyons of concrete.

Sunday afternoons are often "celebrity time" at Sweet Basil. Red Prysock, the torrid saxman, was there at a table with friends, having a good time on the town. So was Joya Sherrill, managing to look forty-ish although she sang with Duke Ellington around 1945. Her "Kissing Bug" was a jukebox favorite of mine as World War II ground to a halt.

Charles Linton, who sang with Chick Webb as early as 1932, came to the microphone for a thirties rendition of "Memories of You" that brought tears to my eyes. He was looking great, wearing a rose-colored turban and sporting a white linen suit, and told me he had played a role when Ella Fitzgerald hit the scene with Webb's orchestra. "I told him I'd quit if he didn't let Ella come with the band," Linton said.

Finally, according to Linton, Webb let the young singer join the band for two weeks, without pay. You know the rest of that story.

Sweet Basil, by the way, is a comfortable place that is intimate, almost to a fault. Our table touched against Doc's music stand. The room was jammed and it took some agility to wiggle through the people to the restrooms, which aren't much larger than broom closets. But it all adds up to "atmosphere." On the plus side, the jazz is as personal as it can get.

Doc's program included "I Thought About You," "Don't Worry About Me," "Love You Madly," "Drop Me Off In Harlem," "New Orleans," "Wolverine Blues," "Emaline," "Muskrat Ramble," "I Got It Bad," "Sophisticated Lady," "Do Nothin' Till You Hear From Me," "It Don't Mean a Thing If It ain't Got That Swing," "Sweet Lorraine," "I've Got a Feeling I'm Falling," "Willow Weep For Me" and "Just You, Just Me."

When Doc sang "New Orleans" and "Sweet Lorraine" it was as though he was singing it to us, though we knew it wasn't quite that way. When his trumpet soared on "Wolverine Blues" I thought I could feel the air from the bell of his horn, though I knew I really couldn't. That's why I prefer intimate jazz to a Las Vegas extravaganza.

We left at 6 p.m., as the combo began "I Guess I'll Get the Papers and Go Home."

The bus depot is a haven for some wild-looking guys and we didn't want to spend an hour or two with them while waiting for a later bus.

# The Metropole

It would be sinful for me to recall my jazz memories in print without including something about the Metropole.

The Metropole, on noisy Seventh Avenue in New York, was the most exciting jazz venue in the whole city in the mid-fifties. That was my experience, at least, when I attended sessions there by Red Allen, Buster Bailey, Cozy Cole, Zutty Singleton and some other greats, plus some near-greats.

Allen had been a favorite of mine a long time and it was good to hear him again, this time in a place large enough (unlike Chicago's Garrick Stage Bar) for me to sit back and relax.

The bands at the Metropole played on the back bar, along the cafe's north wall. It was a long, narrow building that seemed to date back to around World War I and it didn't have much in the way of glitzy fixtures. There were large mirrors along the south wall and the restrooms were upstairs. This detail comes to mind because once, around 1955, I went to the men's room and was surprised to see clarinetist Sol Yaged, a Metropole hired hand, standing at the mirror to shave. It was late afternoon and he had an early show.

Allen was a show in himself. His trumpet playing was still on target, losing none of its punch since I'd seen him in Chicago.

Singleton was a legend, about 60 at the time, who had learned the jazz trade around New Orleans and played with Louis Armstrong and Earl Hines around 1929. I was familiar with him through his records and had seen him in the 1943 movie, "Stormy Weather," with Lena Horne. It was nice to see him "live."

Bailey, an ace reedman who had played with Fletcher Henderson as early as 1924, had impressed me with John Kirby's polite jazz combo and with his recordings for Lionel Hampton. Bailey studied music with Benny Goodman when they were youths. Buster was ranked up there with BG in technique, though he had a thinner tone than Goodman.

"I Know That You Know" was a finger-busting solo by Bailey that I knew from a Hampton disc. One night at the Metropole, around 1957, I asked Buster to play it for me. He responded in the next set, using a bass clarinet to put the old number in new wrappings. It was superb.

Cole, who struck me as being quite a gentlemen as well as a terrific tubster, was riding the good fortune of a hit, "Topsy," in 1958. I preferred him to Singleton because, at age 49, he was more a swing drummer than a New Orleans stylist. He had, in fact, studied at Juilliard and ran a school for drummers in partnership with Gene Krupa for a while.

I was in New York for the Labor Day weekend in 1958 and, naturally, spent a lot of time at the Metropole while bunking at the nearby Century Hotel. There weren't many customers on the holiday afternoon but, as always, there was fine jazz.

Roy Burnes, who had been with the Goodman band at the World's Fair in Brussels, was playing drums that day with, I think, a group led by Yaged. Sol, of course, is known for being able to play Goodman's style to near perfection. He was always showing up at the Metropole.

Burnes told me "what a thrill" it was to play with Goodman that May as the band toured Sweden, Denmark, Germany, Switzerland, Austria, and the Netherlands prior to its week-long engagement in Belgium. The last time I saw

Burnes was on Goodman's TV special, "Swing Into Spring," on Apr. 10, 1959.

The Metropole was a haven for go-go dancers when I went by it in recent years. But my memories linger on, including the night former Ellington trumpeter Louis Metcalf played there with a group that included drummer Shadow Wilson, an ex-Basieite. It was a good blend with Metcalf's low register solos and Wilson's soft brushwork.

The best night, though, was in January of 1963 when I saw Woody Herman at the Metropole.

I had flown into New York on business, arriving at Idlewild just as a snowstorm became a blizzard. I took a taxi to my hotel, north of Central Park, dropped off my bags and hurried to the subway. It was snowing hard around Times Square and I wished I had taken the advice of a co-worker who had urged me to bring galoshes.

As I sloshed my way into the Metropole it just about blew my mind to see Herman's full band, with Joe Newman as an added attraction, strung out the length of the bar. It was one of Woody's best bands, according to ex-sidemen recalling it at the "Early Autumn" reunion at Newport Beach.

The band was definitely in top form, as I recall it from the distant past, with a huge Saturday night crowd. The only drawback, drummer Jake Hanna recalled in 1993, was trying to play without seeing his reflection in the mirrors.

One of Herman's former road managers remembered that the band did "terrific" business during the gig and that the King of Swing was one of its appreciative patrons.

BG asked Herman how, in what was a bad period for big bands, he could draw such large, enthusiastic crowds.

"It's easy," Woody explained. "I do it with mirrors!"

# The London Scene

I have a stock answer when someone asks if I have been to London. "Yes," I say. "I celebrated my 19th birthday there (Nov. 21, 1944) with the buzz bombs going off to add to the excitement."

My weekend in London didn't include any jazz. But I gained a lot of respect for what the Londoners had to put up with during the war. I consider London my favorite among cities I've visited in Europe over the years. Jazz is very popular there. I have fond memories of what I've heard during seven visits since the war.

Ronnie Scott's club, at 47 Frith street, was at the top of my "must see" list in 1976, the first time I had returned to London since the forties. Scott was there, playing some tasty sax and telling some great one-liners. Dizzy Gillespie was the headliner, aided by a hard-driving bass player named Ben Brown.

The club was larger than I expected, with tables arranged in tiers so the customers can see the musicians as well as hear them play. Dizzy was in typical form, meaning he was exciting, unpredictable at times and right on the mark with his up-tilted trumpet.

Millie and I got to Scott's early, to make certain we had seats. It was a few hours before very much happened, except for Scott's puns and his noodlings on sax. One of the jokes had been lifted from Frank Sinatra, who might have gotten it from Milton Berle. It had to do with Scott's first visit to "the states" and the bad luck he had doing some traditional things. "I went to see the Grand Canyon," he quipped, "and it was closed!"

We were at Scott's two other times, once to see McCoy Tyner and the other time for Joe Pass.

We had seen both of them in Chicago and, in particular, I enjoyed Pass. He was the best of current guitarists, along with Bucky Pizzarelli, who is also top-notch. I'd like Tyner better if he had a lighter touch, but wouldn't expect him to change his style on my account.

Scott's club features some excellent British jazzmen in warm-up sessions. Brian Pembroke played fine tenor one night, in advance of Tyner's show. On another occasion, tenorman Tommy Whittle played an uptempo "Autumn Leaves" that was so good I don't expect to ever forget it. It was a masterpiece in subtle, yet driving, swing that was delivered much like "Pres."

In 1988, Millie and I were at Pizza Express to see Wild Bill Davison, who played many years with our friend, Art Hodes. Bill and Art, both around 80 at the time, had experienced a falling out over something rather small. We weren't there with olive branches, but it was nice to hear Bill say something cordial about Art when we mentioned his name.

We had gotten acquainted with Bill's bass player, an American who'd played all over Europe for about 15 years, on the sidewalk outside the club. We helped him get through the door with his bass, as a matter of fact, and wished him well as he descended the stairway into the innards of the room where the band-stand is located. The bandstand is small, as one would expect, but the club was larger and nicer than I had anticipated.

Bill's band was comprised of Europeans or expatriates, and they played the tunes one would expect from Wild Bill Davison, the jazz legend. "I had to move back to the states," Bill told someone, in his booming voice. "The booze and the cigarettes got so expensive over here I couldn't afford to buy them!"

We had a few drinks. I got a snack of some delicious Stilton cheese, served with hard crackers, and Millie sampled some pizza. Then we moved on to the 100 Club, on Oxford Street, to hear Art Farmer. We bypassed Ronnie Scott's on the trip, though it was nearby in Soho, because he was featuring an avant garde combo that wasn't my cup of tea.

We'd been to the 100 Club before, in 1981. We happened to be in London when Prince Charles and Lady Di tied the knot amid the most spectacular fireworks the city had seen since the Battle of Britain. The 100 Club happened to be at the other end of the block from New Berner's Hotel, where we were staying, and it turned out to be a fun-type place. It's located under street level, like so many good jazz clubs, and was so informal we were told to go to the storage room to get our own chairs.

During the earlier visit, Sonny Stitt and Red Holloway provided the entertainment with a night of splendid saxophone solos and duets. They did "Just the Way You Look Tonight" at racetrack tempo, slowing down for some soft-toned ballads later in the set. They'd been touring Europe a while, working with local rhythm sections, and had their act together to a fare-the-well.

Stitt played "Lover Man" as well as I'd heard it done, including Benny Carter's intricate rendition.

(It was a treat a few years later, after Stitt's death, to hear Holloway do the same tune in Burlington, employing what I recalled as some of Sonny's delicate inflections).

Farmer, also backed by European musicians, proved to be the virtuoso I'd expected. He played with more warmth than most of the modernists, using fluegelhorn on most of his solos. His program included "Isfahan" and "Something to Live For," along with some other numbers from his 1987 release called "The Music of Billy Strayhorn," and seemed pleased when I told him I'd bought the tape in Chicago. (Contemporary Records 5C 14029).

All of London is cosmopolitan, of course, but it's educational and sometimes amusing to rub elbows with jazz fans from here, there and everywhere in the city's clubs. They all speak English, at least enough to get by, and it's encouraging to find how many young Europeans, such as some Swedish girls seated near us, appreciate and understand jazz.

Before leaving London in '88 there was an opportunity to go to a place called Pizza On the Park, near Hyde park, where jazz has been featured in recent years.

Pizza On the Park, assuming it still has the same music policy, is a place no visitor to London should miss if his or her taste tends toward jazz. It is a beautiful club, with thick carpeting and oversized chairs and sofas, with only as much illumination as the law requires. The kind of place, in other words, where one might expect to see a movie star, some diplomats or, perhaps, royalty.

The night we were there the music was provided by an almost endless number of superb London pianists. None of the performers had marquee names, but all of them were as good as I'd expect to hear at a jazz festival in the United States. As the parade of talent continued I got to wondering if everyone in London played jazz piano.

One of the pianists, Ian Wright, played "Teach Me Tonight" with a ringing tone, something like George Shearing might do it, as a woman who'd been with Syd Lawrence's popular dance band sang it. Two great performances from, I fear, two artists I'll never hear again.

I've heard some fine jazz in Paris, in Rome, in Zurich and in Amsterdam, but when it comes to jazz in Europe there's no place that rivals London. It is, in overall terms, probably the most fascinating city on earth.

# April in Paris

In Paris, where jazz is a tonic to many, my wife and I went to a cavernous place called the Slow Club, where a "hot jazz sextette" led by clarinetist Rene Franc was doing brisk business three levels below the sidewalk.

My command of French is nil, except for the key menu terms and the realization that an emergency exit is "a sortie." Also, of course, I know that in Paris all things are "nord," "sud," "est" or "ouest" of Notre Dame.

All the tunes played by Franc, who performed ably in the Matty Matlock realm, were American. Such numbers as "China Boy," "Sweet Sue" and "Tiger Rag" plus some standards by Gershwin, Ellington and Porter.

It didn't take long to get acquainted at the Slow Club. The musicians and the club's staff seemed to appreciate an American's delight as their musicians played his country's music in mid-April, 1988.

The combo was quite proficient, and inspired. It was, in fact, about on par with the house bands at Eddie Condon's in the eighties, not counting the nights when such well-known jazzmen as Billy Butterfield or Al Grey sat in.

Dancing was a big thing at the club with the French jitterbugs rivaling the frantic gyrations by New Yorkers at Roseland and the Savoy a half-century ago. The dancers were good enough to be professionals and perhaps some of them were.

The next afternoon, in a quiet cafe with a grand piano, it was a treat to hear new interpretations of familiar tunes. They included a ragtime version of "Blue Moon" that just about wiped me out.

I tried to talk to the pianist. He tried to talk to me. Nothing worked. So we gave up, rather quickly, and I was satisfied to sit down and hear him play.

No translation was necessary as the Frenchman stroked the keyboard, from a laid-back "Stella By Starlight" with just a bit of ornamentation, to a be-bopish "Lullaby of Birdland."

Parisian entertainment guides listed several jazz clubs, most of them tough for us to find and all of them with 9 or 10 p.m. showtimes. One club, where Mal Waldron had played piano in recent years, was "ferme" during our August visit as many people were fleeing Paris for coastal vacations.

Our best bet in several visits in the eighties was the modern Meridien Hotel, where the staff speaks English for the most part and the jazz is eclectic. We've seen an African band there and several combos and large ensembles staffed by superb local musicians. One of the players, who reminded me of Pete Rose in appearance, impressed me with his unusual capacity to play saxes, flute *and* trombone. He was as good as most anyone I'd expect to hear in "the states."

Claude Bolling has a first-rate big band in Paris. But we didn't have any luck finding it, because of a language barrier I couldn't handle. Once, when Bolling was advertised as being in a Left Bank club, I phoned to verify the showtime. The man answering the phone late in the afternoon spoke English but said he either couldn't or wouldn't. Such treatment from people who could do better was very rare, in our experience, in Paris over the years. Usually, jazz seems to bring people together. But I suppose some people in Paris have gotten their fill of tourists who are ignorant about their language.

I still think Paris has a lot of jazz clubs that are worth exploring. If there's a next time I'll do whatever homework it takes, at least to see the Bolling band. It plays some Ellington nearly as well as the Duke did.

During a visit in Amsterdam we found a young guy playing excellent piano, most of it modern stuff, in a loft at a small cafe near the Pulitzer Hotel. In Madrid, there happened to be a jazz club next to our hotel near the American Embassy. The combo was from South America and was comparable to what wed expect at SOB's in New York.

In Montreal, where the prevailing French language has never been a problem for us, we were very impressed by pianist Oliver Jones at the Queen Elizabeth Hotel. Also, the club operated by bassist Charlie Biddle, who frequently plays with Jones, always has good jazz.

There is, in summary, no way I can feel "foreign" toward people in other lands who, while I can't understand most of what they say and write, have as much love for Ellington, Gershwin and "China Boy" as I do.

# Lush Life

Calypso din from one of the glittering lounges was, oddly, the last music heard by the some 1,500 hipsters departing the M/S Seaward at Miami after toe-tapping jazz cruise in November, 1988.

More than 30 top-flight jazzmen, plus vocalists Juanita Hall, Louise Tobin and Meredith d'Ambrosio were on the syncopated voyage. Luscious food and bubbling cocktails were served almost around-the-clock. Pianist John Eaton, during a soiree in one of the bars, termed the floating festival "Lush Life."

Jazz flowed from stages at opposite ends of the new, glistening vessel. Oscar's Piano Bar, thoughtfully deployed amidships, was a busy watering hole for anyone limp from exposure to jazz belted out by the likes of Al Grey, Buddy Tate, Flip Phillips, Scott Hamilton, Dan Barrett, Kenny Davern and Peanuts Hucko in the Stardust and Cabaret lounges.

Oscar's was staffed nightly by Tommy Flanagan, Eddie Higgins and Eaton. Other keyboard men making elegant sounds on the gently-rolling ship included John Bunch, Dick Hyman and Norman Simmons. Mel Powell was there, too, but a health problem kept him from displaying his wares.

There were rhythm players galore. Bassists included Bob Badgely, Milt Hinton, Major Holley and Frank Tate. Howard Alden, Joe Cohn, Chris Flory and Henry Johnson filled the air with melodies from their guitars. The tub-thumping fraternity was represented by Gus Johnson, Ray McKinley, Gerryck King, Jackie Williams and Chuck Riggs.

Terry Gibbs was on board with his vibes and, for just a bit, on piano. Joe Williams pretty much dominated the scene everywhere he went crooning ballads and shouting the blues.

The Seaward, only afloat a few months, was - except for the surprising absence of trumpet players - staffed in great fashion for its inaugural jazz cruise to Jamaica, the Cayman Islands and a tip of Mexico. Celebrated jazz pundits from New York and the West coast were in front row perches to absorb all they could of the hundred-plus hours of scheduled and impromptu sessions. Most of the jazz was, appropriately enough for a floating festival, in the realm known as "mainstream."

Powell, Hucko and McKinley were together for the first time in 44 years, reviving a World War II combo known as "the Uptown Hall Gang" while they were with Maj. Glenn Miller's Army Air Force band. Hucko confirmed that he could still blow mightily with his licorice stick. McKinley was still able to play, at age 78, but offered no threat to his current favorite, Duffy Jackson, or the drummers on board.

Powell had, unfortunately, been ordered by his doctor to avoid the piano for several months while under treatment for a muscular disorder. He was, however, the most popular man on board as he traveled the ten-deck ship on an electric cart. He organized a piano concert, moderated a panel discussion and found time to patronize the ship's tinkling casino, appearing to have remarkable skill.

I must have logged five soft-carpeted miles a day to digest all the music I could hear, including a least eight renderings of "Body and Soul" from port to port. Higgins did it at waltz tempo. Grey did it in a memorable duet around 2 one morning, off the Cuban coast, with Flanagan. Hucko and Gibbs played it during a salute to Benny Goodman. One of the guitarists, either Alden or Cohn, did it with such feeling it nearly choked me up.

All the fare wasn't so sweet. Phillips, alternately honking like Jacquet or Gonsalves and cooing in the style of Lester Young, went through "Just Friends" in what must have been record time. He edged Tate in a battle of the tenors, according to my unofficial tally of the hoots, whistlings and foot stompings from the crowd.

Davern played brilliantly one night, in particular, along with Bunch, Alden, Holley and Riggs. It was their first time as a group, John mentioned, but they sounded as though they had rehearsed for a week. Davern was especially impressive in low register, reminding me of Buster Bailey and also the great Edmond Hall.

Barrett and Alden, two of the best young talents in jazz, reprised some of John Kirby's chamber room jazz. The group, with drummer Riggs and altoist Chuck Wilson, could have used a pianoman to emulate Billy Kyle. But they sounded fine on such familiar Kirby material as "I May Be Wrong." They also offered some warm-blooded jazz with such flaming entrees as Ellington's "Cottontail" and Buck Clayton's "Chocolate Chip."

Hamilton's combo seemed to be the most well-knit and consistent of all the groups on the ship. "Scott is an excellent leader," Bunch told me. The smooth rhythm section had worked together in New York and on tours for a couple of years. All of Hamilton's solos were outstanding, especially a fast "Whispering" that brought Don Byas to mind and, at tenorman Tate's request, a fuzzy-toned "You've Changed."

Bunch, Eaton, Higgins, Hyman, Simmons and Flanagan, who was a replacement for Dave McKenna, were featured in a "piano spectacular" that was emceed by Powell. The 90-minute program was moved along by most of the bass and guitar players on the cruise, providing B-flat interludes for continuity as the pianists came and went.

My favorite numbers included Bunch doing Charlie Parker's "Au Privave," Eaton's "Love For Sale," that was somehow wrapped around "C Jam Blues," Flanagan's dulcet "Lament," an Irving Berlin medley by Hyman and a "St. Louis Blues" in which Higgins invented some new keyboard sounds.

Hyman, with a bag of licks that embraced some Tatumesque runs, played two hour-long jazz history concerts, from ragtime to Broadway. His programs, presented with what seemed to be controlled enthusiasm, included Bix's

"In a Mist," Juan Tizol's "Caravan" and a dozen or so shouts, stomps and rags.

Hinton, known as "the Judge," presided at the final jam session the night before the Seaward docked without, someone in authority announced, the record-breaking amount of stiff beverages that had been dispensed at the bars.

The last-ditch stand in the Cabaret got rolling as Flory, Hamilton, Grey and Tate scratched the surface of things to come with a laid-back "Tickle Toe."

Next, there was a ballad medley with enough sugary choruses to lace the ship crew's coffee well into 1989.

Bunch led off with a frothy "Why Shouldn't I?" and Higgins followed up with an insinuating "Prelude to a Kiss." Al Grey's son, Mike, impressed with a sliphorn solo on "Lush Life" that was sublime.

Flanagan and Phillips got together on a soft, marvelous "All Too Soon." Simmons replied with a tasty "If I Should Lose You." Tate dug into his repertoire for "Polka Dots and Moonbeams." Hyman did credit to "These Foolish Things." Al Grey ended the medley, doing well enough to earn his air fare from Europe with a witty, buzz-muted "Don't Blame Me."

Brooks, an eyeful from New Orleans with a background in church music, followed Hucko and Gibbs on stage after their "Air Mail Special" just about set fire to the ship's carpet. She belted out "Birth of the Blues" with enough gusto to keep the cheering jazz fans on their feet.

Phillips, who hadn't tarried far, returned for a romp through "Limehouse Blues," followed by Holly's show-stopping humor as he bowed and hummed through "Angel Eyes."

The session ended when Williams came on for a mellow set that began with "Little Boy Blue." He cranked the tempo up a notch for "You Can Depend On Me," with lift from Alden's guitar. Williams then invited Phillips to make it a perfect threesome for a soft, slow and gorgeous "Old Folks."

The entire week was, as one of the jazz buffs put it, "a preview of what I hope heaven is like."

# In a Mist

My wife and I were at the Stage Deli for a late snack, shortly after arriving in New York. We drummed up a conversation with a college girl from Ohio who asked what we planned to entertain us in "the Big Apple."

"We'll probably take in a stage show," I said. "I know we'll go to some jazz clubs in the Village."

"Oh," she responded. "I guess you don't have jazz out in Iowa."

"Oh, I shot back, "but we do. Glenn Miller was born in Iowa and Bix Beiderbecke was from just up the river from where we live. You know about Bix?"

That changed the subject to, I think, the weather. It was starting to snow and our hotel was three blocks away. There wasn't time to explain that a lot of Iowans enjoy jazz. But I have to admit that jazz clubs in Iowa are nearly as rare as silos in Central Park. We thrive mostly on one-nighters.

The next night, a Monday, found us crammed into a booth at Sweet Basil to hear the explosion known as the Gil Evans band. The avant garde ensemble, driven by two drummers and a howling synthesizer, played some of the loudest and most exciting stuff I ever heard. Tambourines, whistles, screeching trumpets, honking saxes. You name it, they had it.

But I still had Bix on my mind.

I thought of him when, for a few minutes, the brass, the rhythm men and tuba player Howard Johnson went silent to let Evans be heard at the keyboard.

He could play wonderful piano, or other keyboard instruments, when so inclined. It was like hearing church music after a head-on crash.

It's odd, I suppose, that Gil Evans made me think of Bix Beiderbecke. But they were both great musicians and, in their own way, trailblazers in jazz. They both epitomized the improvisations I enjoy in jazz. That night, more than 1,000 miles from home on the Mississippi, Evans triggered memories of a long-ago riverboat jazzman named Bix. The man who wrote "In a Mist."

Bix was born Mar. 10, 1903, at Davenport. He died Aug. 6, 1931, on Long Island, at age 28. But I think the influence of Leon Bismarck Beiderbecke is still being felt by adventuresome jazz musicians, such as the late Gill Evans.

Part of the reason Bix is still revered is because, with his premature death, a cult has followed in his wake. There is an annual festival in his honor at Davenport. His likeness is painted the size of a billboard a few blocks from where the SS President, launched in the mid-twenties, has been docked in recent years. Bix souvenirs are sold around town 12 months a year.

There is no doubt about the reality of Bix's talent. But his stature has been enhanced by some myths and the fact that the number of his recordings, compared with Ellington or Goodman, was preciously few.

Just about any platter by Bix is "a collector's item." His gold-plated cornet, a Stradivarius model dated 1927 with "Bix" engraved on the bell, will assume the status of crown jewels when placed in a Davenport museum for perpetual display.

"In a Mist" is surely one of the most beautiful compositions in jazz. Along with "Candlelights" and "Davenport Blues," it contributed to a jazz suite played by Bunny Berigan that is a classic. (The suite, with five Beiderbecke numbers, was reissued as an LP in 1990 by RCA/Bluebird as Vol. III of "The Complete Bunny Berigan, 9953-1-RB).

"In a Mist" had an auspicious beginning when it was introduced at Carnegie Hall. Bix had tinkered with the melody a long time, according to Les Swanson of Moline, Ill. , who was in a band with the tune's composer.

Swanson said Bix would "doodle with the chords" before the band would play. Then, during the intermission, he would likely be back at the piano as his bandmates went to the bar. Bix called the number his MF chords, "mit feeling."

He had nearly as much trouble finding a title for the composition as he did putting the chords together, Swanson said in an interview for The Quad-City Times. Bix was back in Davenport a while in the late twenties and played the tune for relatives and friends.

"That's the problem," Bix said when asked what he called the number, which some believed was influenced by Debussy. "I've been kicking it around in my mind and can't think of anything. I'm in a fog about it."

Someone suggested "In a Fog" for the title. "No," Bix said. "That doesn't fit the mood." Someone mentioned "Mist," Swanson reported. That was it.

Swanson said Paul Whiteman liked the tune well enough to unveil it at the opening of his orchestra's tour in 1928. Three grand pianos were rolled onto the stage, Swanson related, and Bix came down from the brass section to play along with Roy Bargy and Lennie Hayton.

The tune was a hit and was recorded by Bix a short while later. It is still popular with many jazz pianists. Ralph Sutton, in particular, has done it "mit feeling" in recent years.

Bix was a modernist, as attested by his exciting solo on Whiteman's 1928 recording of "Sweet Sue." There were other fine musicians in Whiteman's ensemble but they sounded backward compared with Beiderbecke. On liner notes for an LP of Bix's music, critic George Avakian noted that the "Sweet Sue" solo was played with a derby mute on a day the cornetist was "in bad shape." It was, however, one of the finest muted choruses Bix ever played, he opined.

If Bix had lived another 20 years he might have helped propel such innovators as Ellington and Stan Kenton to even greater heights. But those of us who revere Bix must be content to hear such recordings as "Goose Pimples" and "Riverboat Shuffle." Thank you, Mr. Edison, wherever you are.

Few of this era's jazz figures remember Bix first-hand. Art Hodes assured me that he was "as good as they say he was." He wasn't a forceful soloist compared with some others, Art recalled. "He didn't play loud, just great."

Otis Ferguson noted that Bix made his horn "a flexible and eloquent instrument for a personal kind of jazz that had terrific gust in it and rang clear as bells."

Ferguson added: "No one has ever had a more plunging jazz rhythm, or developed such varied syncopations with such complete lack of strain and screaming.

"It takes time," he wrote, "but it is worth the time to find out that Bix's playing grows on you, a hundred times on a million turntables, without wearing out any more than a healthy plant wears out, a perfect thing in nature, and evergreen." (From a 1940 writing not published until "The Otis Ferguson Reader" came out in 1982).

Bix's inspired cornet solos, seeming to soar even in low register, sound as buoyant now on LP or CD as they did when Otis Ferguson wrote about him more than a half-century ago.

But it was the tantalizing "In a Mist," almost always played as a piano solo, that kept coming back to me that night in 1987 at Sweet Basil. Even while the wild sounds erupted by Gil Evans went off a few steps away.

# Butter and Toots

Some of the jazzmen I admired over the years were very able players but didn't gain fame beyond the inner circle of jazz musicians and serious fans.

I enjoyed Ernie Felice, for instance, who played accordion with Benny Goodman's combo in the late forties, and trumpeter Bobby Burnet with Charlie Barnet's band.

Ernie could really swing, without wasting a lot of notes in his terse solos. He wasn't who George Shearing had in mind, most likely, when he defined a perfect gentleman as "a fellow who owns an accordion but never plays it."

Burnet's best record, I thought, was Barnet's "I Can't Get Started," etched in 1942. He played a fine solo on muted horn and managed to avoid anything hinting an imitation of Bunny Berigan's masterpiece. I admired Burnet's originality and good taste, also his tone.

I was in the Panther Room in 1943 when trombonist Quentin Jackson dropped his mute on the floor while playing with Cab Calloway's band. I was seated a few feet from the bandstand and retrieved it for him, earning a nod and "thanks." It was, I guess, equivalent to a kid nuts about baseball picking up something a major leaguer had dropped.

Cab's band was great that night, with Illinois Jacquet going wild on "Flying Home." The band had great precision and discipline. It also had a nifty floor show with eight or ten dazzling, long-stemmed beauties in what Cab referred to as "a Black Market Revue."

"Butter" Jackson played section work that night, for the most part. I kept my eye on him tying to learn what made a swing band tick.

Jackson died Oct. 2, 1976, at age 67. He was playing on Broadway in "Guys and Dolls" at the time. He wasn't a jazz legend, of course, but he had played with Don Redman, McKinney's Cotton Pickers, Lucky Millinder, Count Basie, Duke Ellington and Charlie Mingus. A good list of credentials, I'd say.

I got to thinking about Jackson again a few years ago when a picture of him, taken by Milt Hinton in the thirties, appeared on the cover of The Mississippi Rag. It was an excellent shot of several of Calloway's sidemen in dressy clothes waiting for a train or a bus.

Jackson must have been an excellent musician, judging from his background, though no Jack Teagarden or Lawrence Brown as a soloist. All musicians can't be stars, it occurred to me when I heard of his death. I'm glad to have had the chance to be polite to him, even in a trivial way. He was, I think, the first noted jazzman I ever talked to.

I never met Nuncio ("Toots") Mondello, or heard him play in person, but was a fan of his because of the beautiful tone he got from his alto sax.

You knew it was Toots when you heard him, doing a solo or dominating a reed section. I had a 78-rpm record by Toots, "Shades of Jade," in which his tone rivaled just about anyone's except for Johnny Hodges, Benny Carter or Willie Smith.

It bothered me in 1988 when Sol Yaged mailed me a clipping from the New York Times reporting that Toots might get the bounce from his apartment house.

"A French singer with a pet pigeon lives there," it was noted. "So do a former vaudeville female impersonator, a saxophonist who played with Benny Goodman and a woman who began her theater career as a cat."

Toots, it appeared, was going to be evicted along with the others from the Whitby, at 325 West 45th Street, when the owners turned the building into a cooperative. The Whitby had been home to generations of struggling chorus girls, traveling jazz musicians and Broadway hopefuls since 1923.

"When I first moved here they were tickled just to have us," said Mondello, who had moved into the Whitby in 1934. "Now, it's uncomfortable living here. You don't feel like it's your home."

I wrote Toots, telling him how much I enjoyed his music over the years, mostly with Goodman, and mentioning "Shades of Jade."

"Thank you for your kind and complimentary letter," he responded on Feb. 15, 1988. He said he couldn't remember playing with BG at a Carnegie Hall concert on Oct. 6, 1939, though his name was on an LP of the performance. "Is it possible that there is some mistake?", he asked. "I was never much of a collector of the recordings I played on."

"Shades of Jade" was one of six solos he wrote for Robbins Music, Toots related. "I recorded all six with just Claude Thornhill on piano and Nick Fatool on drums. God knows whatever happened to them. The label was Royal."

Mondello died in December, 1992, of cancer at age 81.

"Mr. Mondello, who was known as Toots, was the principal alto saxophone player in Benny Goodman's band on the national radio show, 'Let's Dance,' in 1934 and 1935 and again in the early 1940's," it was reported in The Times. "He was also a well known studio musician who played on network radio and television for stars including Kate Smith, Ed Sullivan and Milton Berle."

Toots was born in Boston, his obituary said, and was playing solos with his father's dance band when he was eight years old. At 17, he was assistant leader for Mal Hallett and he later played for Buddy Rogers and Joe Haymes.

With Goodman, my favorite solo by Toots was on "Beyond the Moon," a number arranged by Fletcher Henderson that was, according to Russ Connor, first titled "Toot's Dream." It was recorded by Columbia on Nov. 22, 1939, the same day Mildred Bailey recorded "Peace Brother" with the band, also with a fine solo by Toots.

Mondello didn't leave any survivors, according to The Times, only a legacy of top-notch music.

# Feelings

Perhaps the most redeeming thing about "today's music" is the fact that it is so aptly named. It is, after all, here today and gone tomorrow, with only a few notable exceptions.

That isn't so, on the other hand, with hundreds of songs that have earned the status of "standards" in the books of the endearing vocalists, such as Ella Fitzgerald and Frank Sinatra, the Broadway stars, the top-flight jazz players and the nation's dance bands.

The popular music with lasting impact, composed by such American greats as Cole Porter, Duke Ellington and George Gershwin, is still loved by millions and remains very much in style.

Hoagy Carmichael's "Stardust," penned in 1929, is apparently going to live forever. Decades of longevity, at least, can also be predicted for, to cite just a few, such musical gems as Johnny Green's "Body and Soul," Irving Berlin's "Blue Skies," Jerome Kern's "Smoke Gets In Your Eyes" and Harold Arlen's "Stormy Weather." Such numbers are equally great, it seems, with lyrics or as instrumentals.

Why are these songs still so enjoyable when so many of the tunes written by today's composers are headed for oblivion as quickly as last year's style in women's hats?

The best answer I heard from an expert source was voiced by Art Hodes who, at age 85, was still in demand as a pianist, bandleader and jazz lecturer in New Zealand, Australia, Canada, Europe and across the United States.

Hodes, whose credentials included concerts in Carnegie Hall as well as gigs in many of the nation's top jazz clubs, said the evergreen aura of "good old days" music is a reflection of its rhythmic qualities. More important, he felt, such music has "feeling" in emotional terms. The kind of feeling not contained in loud, mechanical music that comes up short in cerebral appeal.

One of Hodes' favorite techniques was to play a few bars of something with value, such as Gershwin's "The Man I Love," circa 1925. Then he would remind the audience of the composition's durability on concert stages, in movies and as a number to "jam."

"Today's kids tend to think everything that amounts to much happened after they hit the scene," Art would say, with a laugh, to make his point. "Actually, composers such as Gershwin were more than 30 years ahead of the Beatles."

And their music, more so than that of the rock purveyors, will stand the test of time. That is what Hodes was saying three decades ago. Nothing has happened to prove him wrong.

Hodes didn't discuss new-age music, rock'n roll and today's novelty tunes in bitter fashion. He had to laugh, though, at much of what he heard.

He had seen Hit Parade numbers come and go since the era of Paul Whiteman and Gershwin's "Rhapsody In Blue." Understandably, I think, he had to wince when he heard the label of "genius" applied to composers that, to put it politely, weren't destined for long-term success.

I happened to believe, as Art Hodes did, that people will still be whistling, humming, dancing and listening to songs such as "Stardust" and "The Man I Love" long after those of us with first-hand recollections of Carmichael and Gershwin have departed this planet.

NOTE: This item first appeared on the op-ed page of The Des Moines Register on July 24, 1987. Three of the 24 items I wrote for the Register in that era were, in fact, essays about jazz.

# Tune Talk

The following article was inspired by US Sen. Joe Biden's withdrawal from the presidential campaign when he was caught plagiarizing another politician's speech. It appeared in the Des Moines Register on Oct. 7, 1987:

Back in the pre-Biden era, my only concern about plagiarism (defined by Simon and Schuster as "to take ideas or writings from another and pass them off as one's own") was getting it spelled right.

"It Never Entered My Mind," to quote a 1940 song title by Richard Rogers and Lorenz Hart, that I might someday have to be concerned about the informal stuff I write getting me into a jam.

The situation has changed, as anyone who did not sleep through the past several weeks should know. It appears that a lot of us may need to be, a la Mikhail Baryshnikov, on our toes.

So, "From This Moment On," as Cole Porter rhapsodized some 3 1/2 decades ago, I have pledged to not even write about someone whistling "Dixie" without giving Daniel Decatur Emmett, who penned that anthem in 1859, a precautionary credit line.

I'm fearful, to be candid about it, that if heavy caliber public servants such as Senator Biden can be blown out of the arena by taking such trivial liberties as lifting a few dozen words from someone else's speech, then small fry sounding off in the papers could also get stung for their petty thefts.

"It Could Happen To You," as Johnny Burke and Jimmy Van Husen put it in their mid-forties melody, I realized after Biden went down for the count.

Politicians and those who grind out prose are not, obviously, the only ones vulnerable if the all-out war against plagiarism is fought all the way to its bitter, logical conclusion.

TV weather prophets, for example, had better be ready to give Irving Berlin his full due when forecasting "Blue Skies." Ditto for cases when Harold Arlen's "Stormy Weather" is on the horizon. Or Eugene Ford's "Rain." Don't even mention "Summertime," you weathermen, without giving Mr. Gershwin his due.

Travel agents, likewise, would do well to cite E.Y. Harburg and Vernon Duke, with equal attribution, when suggesting that a client with wanderlust spend "April In Paris." Mention Gene Roland and Jacque Cascales, surely, if sending someone off to "Winter In Madrid."

No restaurateur worth his salt, or his paprika and his oregano, should risk serving "Tea for Two," or even for one, without conspicuous mention of Vincent Youmans on his bill of fare. Don't forget Mr. Berlin when serving up a "Yam."

Couples in a romantic mood should pause long enough to acknowledge that it was James P. Johnson, the stride pianist of roaring twenties reknown, who originated "Old Fashioned Love." Mr. Porter, meanwhile, was a bit more sly when he advised: "Let's Do It."

Certainly, any prudent youngster or adult should "Remember," in the spirit delineated by Mr. Berlin, what happens to those of us who, as Walter Donaldson warned, tell "Little White Lies."

These admonitions could, of course, have rolled along, as characterized by Jerome Kern and Oscar Hamerstein in "Ol' Man River," to this journal's stock market page.

But, for brevity's sake, I'm concluding with the assumption that the senator from Delaware bowed out by, more or less, asking: "What Can I Say After I Say I'm Sorry?"

If his swan song included that sort of humble remorse I hope he was careful, after all he has been through, to give Mr. Donaldson and Abe Lyman credit for their original thought.

# Thanks, Glenn

This book of jazz recollections wouldn't' be complete without some words of appreciation for Glenn Miller.

Miller's pre-war band wasn't a particular favorite of mine because it didn't play a whole lot of good jazz. While BG played "King Porter Stomp" and Basie played "Lester Leaps In" the Miller band was known for its dance music, such as syrupy stuff as "Moonlight Cocktails," and its novelties.

I gained respect for Miller in 1944, though, when his Army Air Force crew played in Europe. The band elevated morale for the GIs and, I am sure, the civilians in Britain who got to see the big, string-augmented ensemble perform.

My outfit, the 106th Infantry Division, spent a month near Oxford prior to being shellacked in the opening round of the Battle of the Bulge. Miller's band, with Mel Powell on piano, Peanuts Hucko playing clarinet and Ray McKinley at the drums, was on the air nightly. We listened in our hut on a $15 radio purchased in a village shop.

The band played Miller's dance tunes, of course. But it also belted out some very respectable jazz, with Bernie Privin getting off some Beriganesque solos. I also enjoyed the "something old, something new, something borrowed, something blue" medleys. One of my favorites included "Londonderry Air," "Shoo-Shoo Baby," "The Way You Look Tonight" and "Blue Danube." Remember that?

I got to London one weekend, hoping to see the Miller band, especially Hucko and Powell. But they had been moved to a safer locale during attacks from buzz bombs and the soaring V-2 rockets. One V-2 that landed miles away shook the Piccadilly Hotel on, I recall, Nov. 19, 1944.

So we kept listening, night after night, until sailing to France, landing at LeHavre on what we calculated to be D-Day "plus 150 days."

I was carrying our radio much of the time, because I loved the music so much. Along with an automatic rifle, my full fieldpack with a horseshoe roll, a gas mask, a trench knife and an extra bag of BAR ammo around my neck.

We never found a wall receptacle for the radio while up front in the Siegfried Line. When the Bulge erupted on Dec. 16, 1944, I threw the radio in a snow-filled ditch along with my gas mask, my overcoat, etc., so I could "travel light." This was the day Maj. Glenn Miller, an Iowa native, disappeared.

I was a POW until Apr. 24, 1945. There were no radios in the prison camps, at least not in the coal mine where 25 of us worked. But I could still hear the music of Glenn Miller in my mind, along with Goodman's "Henderson Stomp" and Ellington's "Cottontail."

Wingy Manone kept running through my head with "Stop that war, them cats are killin' themselves." It was, I guess, the first anti-war song in my generation.

After our liberation, back in LeHavre and Camp Lucky Strike, I was just as anxious for the V-Discs as I was for the pancakes, hot showers and toilet paper.

In 1988, I talked to drummer McKinley on the Seaward during a lull in the jazz cruise. He said something about the morale-boosting mission of Miller's band. The same kind of mission Artie Shaw, Davey Tough, Claude Thornhill, Max Kaminsky and other jazzmen had in the war zones.

"You might wonder if your music really gave us a lift," I said. "Glenn Miller's music ranked right up there with pay-day and mail call as far as I'm concerned."

# Coda

Writing the text of this book, with countless revisions along the way, was a four-month job

When it was finally done, in March of 1994, it seemed like a good idea to top it all off with a definition of jazz. After some thought, it wasn't such a good idea.

There are eight to ten types of jazz, from ragtime to avant garde, depending upon who's counting. The types toward the middle, away from the extremes, tend to be the most enjoyable over the long haul.

Jazz can shout, as it does when played by Maynard Ferguson, or it can whisper as it does with Gary Burton at the vibes.

It seems best, in the final analysis, to be broad-minded about jazz rather than just hear 5 or 10 percent of it.

There is, on the other hand, merit to following the advice of Pinetop Smith, or perhaps it was Thelonious Monk, who recommended: "To each his own."